Praise for Blowing Zen

"A genuine spiritual journey, finding Zen, music, and one's own true self. A lovely spirit blows through this book."

— **Jack Kornfield**, author of *A Path With Heart*

"Ray Brooks's unique and captivating book provides an insightful view of the heart and spirit of Japanese culture and the musician's journey. In sharing his quest, he has enriched my life, and may inspire many others on the paths of music, the ways of Zen."

— **Dan Millman**, author of *Way of the Peaceful Warrior* and *The Life You Were Born to Live*

"*Blowing Zen* is a shining paradigm of positive, life-affirming change. Ray's awakening to the deep, inner song that is Life inspires and gives hope to those searching for their own true path."

— **John Robbins**, author of *Diet for a New America*

"A good book captivates—takes you to a different corner of the world and a different way of thinking. It's one you reach for again and again. *Blowing Zen* is such a book."

— **Todd Shimoda**, author of *365 Views of Mt. Fuji*

"Not since Mickey Hart's *Drumming at the Edge of Magic* has a book so beautifully and eloquently exemplified the connection between spirit and music. *Blowing Zen* is a must-read for any musician or artist needing to manifest that connection."

— **Greg Ellis**, percussionist and co-founder of VAS

Blowing Zen

Finding an Authentic Life

Blowing Zen

Finding an Authentic Life

Ray Brooks

HJ KRAMER INC
TIBURON, CALIFORNIA

*This is a true story. I have changed the names of some of the
people described in it out of respect for their privacy.* R. B.

H J Kramer Inc
P.O. Box 1082
Tiburon, CA 94920

Editor: Nancy Grimley Carleton
Editorial Assistant: Claudette Charbonneau
Cover Design: Jim Marin/Marin Graphic Services
Composition: Classic Typography
Manufactured in the United States of America.
10 9 8 7 6 5 4 3 2 1

Library of Congress Cataloging-in-Publication Data
Brooks, Ray, 1949–
    Blowing Zen : finding an authentic life / Ray Brooks.
        p. cm.
    ISBN 0-915811-85-5
    1. Brooks, Ray, 1949–   . 2. Shakuhachi players Biography.
3. Spiritual biography. I. Title.
ML419.B747A3   2000
788.3'5'092—dc21
    [B]   99-34947
                                                            CIP

For Sakai-san

To Our Readers

The books we publish
are our contribution to an
emerging world based on cooperation
rather than on competition, on affirmation
of the human spirit rather than on self-doubt,
and on the certainty that all humanity is
connected. Our goal is to touch as many lives
as possible with a message
of hope for a better world.

Hal and Linda Kramer, Publishers

Contents

Contents

Foreword

In *Blowing Zen,* the author's reflections on his remarkable adventures in Japan are filled with insight as well as inspiration. This is the story of a modern-day *komuso* ("wandering monk"), whose path to enlightenment is global in scope and whose drive to awaken is amplified only by the sound of the Zen bamboo flute, the shakuhachi.

The origins of the shakuhachi can be traced back to antiquity. From ancient Egypt, this woodwind instrument presumably traveled through Mesopotamia to India and then China, before crossing the Sea of Japan in the sixth century. Like Buddhism itself, the spiritual foundation upon which its practice is based, this unique musical instrument moved from West to East. Now we witness the shakuhachi crossing the Pacific to find fertile ground in the hearts of a new generation in the West.

Ray Brooks has served as one vehicle of this odyssey. Having emerged from the maelstrom of the 1960s to question the very core of his being, Ray discovered some very old answers to some very new questions. With his gaze directed steadily inward, Ray's quest for solutions led him to a doorway that opened to the ancient wisdom of the East. In the pages that follow, an incredible journey unfolds. It is the voyage of one man's self-discovery through the conduit of the shakuhachi. This rustic five-hole flute made from the root of bamboo became a portal through which the author came face-to-face with a wider view of his life and his place in the cosmos.

As a maker of shakuhachi flutes since 1970, at the hub of the informational wheel of this unique tradition, I have been privy to several amazing stories of folks who have encountered shakuhachi completely outside of its traditional context. Many recognized its potential and opened to its special gift. Few, however, have taken the call as earnestly, passionately, and unabashedly as Ray Brooks, who follows its sweet melodic intensity to the ends of the earth in search of a rendezvous with his true self.

Monty H. Levenson
Willits, California

Preface

How did a completely undisciplined child—an utter waster in his twenties, who squandered the best part of his early life in the pubs, wine bars, and nightclubs of London—find himself playing solo concerts in Japan on a Zen flute? For those who know me, this is the question most asked. For those who meet me through my concerts and workshops, this is the part that most intrigues.

This book began as an attempt to respond to that question. Writing it afforded me the opportunity to look back, in appreciation, at the moments of change in my life. It allowed me to remember the people I'd met, and some of the extraordinary paths I crossed, which might otherwise have been forgotten.

I wrote *Blowing Zen* with the hope that at least one person with thoughts of changing his or her life—from whatever walk of life—will be inspired into action.

Ray Brooks
Victoria, British Columbia, Canada

Acknowledgments

I have met many good friends on this journey, who, in some cases unknowingly, helped in all aspects of the creation of this book. I wish to express my special appreciation to Dianne Brooks, for her crystal clear thinking, vital input, insistence on accuracy, and creative editing skills. This book would not have been possible without her.

I am deeply indebted to the following people for assisting me with this project: To Andrea Scott, for her invaluable assistance in the early stages. To Diane Barlee, for her tireless efforts, advice, and constant encouragement. She alone saw "the book" in me from day one. Thank you, Diane. A special thanks to Roslyn Targ, my agent, for putting her well-respected name to my manuscript, and to Hal and Linda Kramer, for allowing *Blowing Zen* to be published by H J Kramer Inc, which, in the publishing world is known as a company of great integrity. To my editor, Nancy Grimley Carleton, for the final touches and suggestions.

My deepest appreciation to Yokoyama Sensei, Akikazu Nakamura Sensei, Yamada Sensei, Sasaki Sensei, and all the teachers I have had the opportunity to study under throughout Japan and India. I thank all of them for their kindness, generosity, and inexhaustible wisdom. All have taught me much more than just music.

Acknowledgments

Special thanks to Jan Phillips, Managing Editor at H J Kramer, and Monique Muhlenkamp, Publicist, as well as Setsuko Iida, Shawn Klemmer, Peter Morgan-Locke, Patti Meadows, David Drysdale, and Peter Ross. My deepest appreciation to Monty H. Levenson for writing the Foreword.

杉
風
之
調

Chapter One
Zen Tourist

The atmosphere in the meditation hall was one of deep calm, but my mind was racing.

Just breathe, I told myself. *One inhale, two exhale, three inhale, four. So this is zazen, Buddha's illustrious cross-legged position. Ahh! My legs are killing me. Breathe . . . just think of nothing. Think of nothing? God, I feel drowsy! What a night that was. Probably only slept an hour. Hope I can get some sleep tonight. One inhale, two exhale . . .*

Thwack!

What the . . . ?

The sharp, smacking sound of a monitor's "helping stick" filled the *zendo,* our meditation hall, ending the delusions of a poor, unsuspecting meditator. Two black-robed monks, as expressionless as androids, patrolled back and forth, each carrying a flat, narrow stick. One circled the shaven-headed "authentics" on the far side of the zendo, while the other circled the "weekend dabblers" on my side. My knees ached, and I was desperate to straighten my legs.

The advertisement in the classified section of the *Japan Times* had read:

> Three-days Zen meditation retreat in Shizuoka.
> In beautiful nature. Foreigner welcome.
> Please call for appointment.

This seemed like an ideal opportunity to visit a Zen temple and participate in zazen firsthand. Excited at the prospect of getting out of Tokyo for a few days and amused by the thought of being lost in the "ethereal mist of Zen," I called and made a reservation.

Over the years, meditation for me usually came about through uninvited moments of awareness, moments when there was no separation between me and what I was doing. Although I'd always respected the value of sitting quietly without any form of visual stimulation, I'd avoided this style of meditation mostly because of my lack of flexibility and my inexperience at sitting for long periods of time.

Anticipating the discomfort of zazen, I practiced for a few days before I left, sitting on the floor in the necessary position whenever I could. It didn't seem so bad in twenty-minute blocks, although admittedly, my back was propped up against the sofa and I did have the odd stretch as I read the newspaper.

Alas, once ensconced in the silent zendo with my throbbing knees, the mist began to lift, taking the novelty with it.

Thwack!

Shit! That was close. I haven't been hit with a stick since primary school. I don't think my knees can stand much more of this. I'll never make it to the bell. God, my mind's all over the place. . . . Breathe, just breathe . . .

2

The stark resemblance between the discipline of the zendo and my primary school brought back poignant memories of my childhood. With the memories came familiar feelings of insecurity and fear. Interested, I didn't chase these feelings away, but just watched to see where they would take me.

Granma was spitting on her hands and flattening my hair in anticipation of my mother's arrival. I could smell her spittle and feel those hard old hands pushing down on my head. "You're a sight for sore eyes, our Raymond," she grumbled. I was six years old and couldn't remember if I'd seen my mother before, having been left with my grandparents when I was only two years old. She was here for a short visit I was told. Three days later she was gone. Two years later she appeared again. Three days later she was gone again. I remember asking Granma why my mother didn't stay and look after me, like Billy's mum.

Granma, old and suffering from dementia, did the best she could with me. She'd seen the backs of seven of her own children and just buried her second husband, so she had very little energy left when it came to disciplining me. She had lived her whole life in the same tiny coal-mining village in the North East of England and, like the locals, Granma was a woman of very few words. Clouts around the ear were about the extent of my training in telling right from wrong. Encouraged to entertain myself so that Granma could have some "peace and quiet," I became popular among my peers, mischief and fun always guaranteed. Indeed, I was one of the most unruly children in the neighborhood and at school in those days.

As far as emotional support, well that was for girls. Granma, ill equipped herself, was incapable of dealing with my feelings of confusion, so I did what most people do every day: I subconsciously buried, dodged, and denied. I could barely tie my shoelaces, yet already I was developing an infinite capacity for self-deception. No one was going to hurt me! Bulletproof was best.

Thwack!

One inhale, two exhale, three . . . four . . . five. God! I'm stiff. . . . I should do yoga. . . .

"So, Mr. Brooks, why are you here today?"

"Well, I thought I'd just check in for a masochistic weekend and rid myself of desire." The desire to rid yourself of desire . . . there's that infinite capacity for self-deception again. So . . . here I am, wall gazing, waiting to be cudgeled by Zen Man. . . . God! I can't wait to walk outside in the garden again . . . .

Suddenly, I heard the sound of padding feet and the rustle of a robe. The monitor was upon me. Quickly, my thoughts rushed back to their cells, scrambling like mischievous inmates in a sanitarium. Resisting the urge to open my eyes, I braced myself and waited. The strike didn't come, only a gentle correction of my sagging posture.

I'd been up since 2:00 AM that morning, unable to sleep with the chorus of six huffing, wheezing, and snoring Japanese businessmen with whom I was sharing a dorm. I gathered that my companions' companies were footing the bill for their retreat. Not an entirely altruistic motive, I was sure. More likely it was to refocus them in order to keep up maximum working efficiency. Finally the noise of their snoring became too much for me, so I had crept outside and walked around the temple grounds in the May moonlight.

I guessed I'd been sitting in zazen now for about forty-five minutes, but it could have been much less. The pain in my knees was now almost unbearable, and the circulation to my feet felt like it had stopped at the ankles. I was beginning to feel slightly panicked about staying in this position any longer. I tried to breathe deeply, hoping to ease the agony, but it was useless. I could think of nothing but the agony in my knees. Consoling myself, I imagined turning around and sticking my legs out in front of me and dangling them over the raised platform I was seated on.

Thwack!

Shit! Zen Man's back.

I could hear the swish, swish, swish of his robe coming closer again. Then silence. I felt the monk's presence behind me. I held my breath and braced myself again, ready to accept a good thumping for the offense of daydreaming about straight legs. The wallop never came. Instead, the monk thoughtfully placed a cushion underneath each knee. A sense of affection bubbled up inside of me, and relief was instant.

Breathing deeply, I began to relax and count again. Without the acute pain, my body became more settled, more concentrated.

Seven inhale, eight exhale, nine inhale . . .

Suddenly the gong was struck, and I was jolted into wakefulness. Had I been dozing? I half-opened my eyes, regained my composure, and surreptitiously glanced at my neighbor, imitating his actions. Rising from our cushions, we carefully climbed off the platform, and facing the opposite row, bowed with palms together. We then turned to our left and began *kinhin,* a slow-motion walking meditation practiced between sitting periods. Following in single-file, my knees and ankles numb, I started to stiffly circle the zendo. I passed the black-robed monk who'd shown me such kindness, and a fondness welled in my chest. I wanted to hug and thank him, but he looked straight through me with an unimpassioned stare. Brilliant! Forty-five minutes into my Zen training, and already I was developing an attachment!

After circling the hall three times, I was back in front of my stack of cushions. I mounted the platform as reverently as possible, conscious of it being a sacred area. The day before I'd been told by a young monk that in ancient times the monks not only meditated on this platform, but also slept and ate on it. Apparently the first thirty centimeters were *under no circumstances* to be touched by one's feet, as this was where the food was once placed and eaten each day. This custom was still practiced, even though the area was now only used for meditation. The monk had also carefully demonstrated exactly how we should mount the cushion in readiness for zazen.

In the second period of sitting my knee pain eased, and I sat in a comfortable silence. My mind was less agitated, almost calm. But at the end of the completed session, the striking of the gong once again startled me.

I spun around and struggled off the cushion, this time accidentally touching the sacred area with my foot—perhaps the first to touch it in one hundred years! I stepped down to the wooden floor, placed my palms together, and bowed center, right, and left. Unfortunately the others bowed center, left, and right. We left the room in single file, each stopping at the door, turning and bowing to a vase full of fresh flowers.

Breakfast was an incredibly complicated affair—the antithesis of fast-food dining. We sat in zazen facing each other in two rows, with twelve people in each row. The monks sat on one side, their heads gleaming and reflecting the light from the fluorescent tubes suspended above us. I sat at the other side with the laymen. On the low tables in front of each of us, wrapped and knotted skillfully in white cloth, was a stack of three bowls. The day before I'd been shown the meticulous and disciplined eating procedure, the head monk assuring me of its importance and value.

"Monk learn all rule, no need mind, only eat, drink." Come to think of it, maybe it wasn't so different from the fast-food experience.

The whole meal was spent in silence. The head monk, like a metronome, set the eating pace. We all had to finish at the same time. In a kind of soporific state and feeling slightly euphoric, I wanted to talk, but contained myself. No one near me spoke English anyway.

Relief came at 7:30 AM, when we were given an hour of free time. After washing, I set off down a winding, cobbled path, through the flawlessly manicured garden, passing plants and trees that had succumbed to the discipline of a Japanese Zen gardener. Rocks and stones were deliberately placed, some surrounded by white gravel that had been raked into ripples of perfection. My eyes were drawn to a few rebellious stones that had escaped onto the path. I wondered if the perfection of the raked gravel symbolized an outward expression of a Zen mind. The stones on the path: unruly thoughts.

The garden projected a look of perfect outer order, and gave the illusion of permanence. Nothing was left to grow wild. Nothing was untended. I felt that it wasn't just a simple matter of skillful aesthetics. The perfection seemed to betray something much deeper about the Japanese people, perhaps an unconscious fear of unpredictable forces. Forces of nature, of humanity, of things beyond their control.

I continued walking, my attention focusing on the sights, sounds, and smells around me. The lack of sleep now appeared to have quieted my mind. In the open air of the garden, there wasn't the familiar weight of past or future, and that constant underlying feeling of self was weakened. It was a glorious day. The early morning sun and clear blue sky invited me to sprawl on the grass and stare to the heavens, but the garden seemed to advocate restraint, almost saying, "Relax, but don't relax."

I stood for a while, listening to a hovering skylark's beautiful song, and then in the background, I caught the faintest sound of a flute. It seemed to be coming from the gazebo near the willow trees. I strolled towards the music. As I neared, I recognized the player. I had asked him for directions to the temple the day before, and he had told me that he, too, was going to the Zen retreat. As we walked together from the bus station, he had asked me all the usual questions—where I came from, what I was doing in Japan, how long I had been in the country, and how long I intended to stay. I answered his questions and then asked if he'd visited this temple before. He said he had, then told me that due to the great pressure of his work he needed to retreat once in a while. His English was almost fluent as a result of having lived and worked in London for several years.

"Ah. Good morning, please join me," he now offered, lowering his flute.

"Hello. Ozawa-san, isn't it?"

"*Hai,* hello. Yes, eh, Mr. Ray, right?"

"Please, just Ray."

"Ah yes, Ray-san."

"I heard the sound of your flute from quite a distance," I told him.

"Oh really, I'm sorry. I'm not a good player," he said apologetically.

"No, no! Your playing fits perfectly with the atmosphere of the place."

"Please sit down, Ray-san. How are you finding the zazen training?"

"Very painful," I responded honestly.

"We Japanese also find it very difficult; if we don't sit in zazen daily, we quickly lose our flexibility," he consoled me. Japanese responses often have this instinctive empathetic quality about them, a quality that saves one from embarrassment or from feelings of inadequacy.

"That's a very unusual flute," I commented. "I can't remember ever seeing one quite like it. It's beautiful."

"Thank you. It's a Japanese bamboo flute. We call it *shakuhachi*. Do you know shakuhachi, Ray-san?"

He held out the flute in front of himself. I vaguely remembered hearing the word before.

"How do you say it?" I asked.

"Sha-ku-ha-chi. Maybe you know it as Japanese Zen flute in your country."

"Sha-ku-ha-chi," I repeated.

"Please," I said, inviting him to demonstrate.

He placed the flute to his lips and blew a deep mysterious tone. Unlike the standard Western flute, this instrument was held vertically and blown from the end.

"*Dozo*. Please," he said, handing the instrument to me and beckoning me to inspect it.

I ran my fingers across its smooth surface and over its seven ridged nodes, grasping the gnarled root at the end.

"It's quite heavy compared to other bamboo flutes," I observed, weighing the instrument in my hand.

"Yes. When it is bored out, the walls are left thick, and we leave the root of the bamboo on the end."

The flute was about two feet long and had a slanted blowing edge at the top. There was a joint in the middle where it could come apart. The end was bell-shaped, with the individual roots of the plant still attached, but clipped in very closely, giving the flute a very primitive and natural look. Four holes were drilled in the front and one at the back. The coloring had a slight golden hue with dark marks at the root end.

"Do you play a musical instrument, Ray-san?" he asked.

"No, not really," I replied, handing the flute back to him. "But when I was eighteen I tried to learn the saxophone for a while, but eventually gave it up."

"Yes. It's difficult to find the time, isn't it?" he said sensitively.

I turned my attention back to the flute.

"Only five holes," I noted aloud.

"Yes, but we can half-hole and produce every note."

"Really?"

"Yes, musically if we only used the five holes, the flute would be very limited, as we'd only be able to play D-F-G-A-C. But, by slightly uncovering the holes, like this . . ."—he began to demonstrate—"we can play all the semitones between them."

"So, you can play the whole chromatic scale?" I asked.

"Yes, and in the hands of a shakuhachi master many microtones can also be achieved."

"It's sounds like a remarkable instrument. Did you make it yourself, Ozawa-san?"

He looked surprised at the suggestion.

"No, much too difficult." He stood up excitedly, and his voice took on a new intensity. "The procedure is quite complicated and takes much experience. First the right kind of bamboo must be found and then carefully dug up from the ground, keeping the surface roots intact. Then, after cleaning and drying, it must be stored out of the sunlight for three to six years, sometimes longer. After it is properly aged, a master maker will go through many complex steps before the flute is ready for playing."

"Are there many shakuhachi makers?" I inquired.

"Few good ones. Like so many Japanese arts, slowly dying, Ray-san."

He offered the flute to me again, and as if handling a telescope, I peered down the red lacquered barrel. It was smooth and shiny, and the bore tapered from the mouthpiece to the root end.

"Dozo, Ray-san. Please try it." I brought the flute to my lips and blew. Nothing, only the sound of air whistling. Ozawa-san expertly corrected the angle of my head and the flute. A barely audible sound emerged.

"*Sugoi,* Ray-san, very good. Most people don't make a sound first try."

"I thought it would have been easier," I admitted, returning the flute to him.

"No, I'm afraid not, Ray-san. The shakuhachi has the reputation of being an extremely challenging instrument to master. Some even say it is one of the most difficult instruments to learn in the world. It takes a lifetime of study."

"Do many Japanese people study it?"

"Sadly, fewer and fewer these days. Young people no longer have the time or discipline that is needed to study the art of shakuhachi. Most of them tend to see it as *furukusai,* or stinking of old," he laughed.

"You mentioned it was a Zen flute. What's the connection to Zen?" I asked.

Without further urging, he went on to tell me how, in the eighteenth and nineteenth centuries, shakuhachi was used as a religious instrument solely by beggar monks called *komuso*.

"Komuso breaks down into three Japanese characters," he said, using his finger to draw each one on the palm of his hand. "*Ko* means emptiness, *mu* is illusion, and *so* means monk. Together they translate into English as 'monks of nothingness and emptiness.' The monks belonged to a Zen Buddhist sect called *Fuke* and chose to live a life of poverty and hardship. In order to survive, they went on pilgrimages, wandering from place to place playing shakuhachi for alms. The sound of the flute reminded the people of the Buddha-Dharma. Unlike other Zen monks who practice sutra chanting and zazen, or sitting meditation, as their discipline, the komuso practiced *suizen*. *Suizen* literally means 'blowing Zen,' and involves the discipline of breath control through the flute. This they achieved by learning to play pieces, which they called meditations. What was required from the monks was not mere technique but the development of strong spirit. So you see, Ray-san, the flute was used in fact as a religious tool."

"Blowing Zen! A tool for blowing Zen!" I said enthusiastically.

"Yes. The monks were trying to put themselves into a state of higher consciousness," he added. It's called *satori* in Japanese. The monks had a saying amongst themselves: *ichi on jobutsu,* or 'enlightenment in one sound.'"

"May I look at the flute again, Ozawa-san?"

He passed it to me, and with renewed interest I examined it again.

"Why is part of the root kept on the end?" I asked.

"Hmmm, well . . . during the last century some who joined the Fuke sect were . . . how can I say? They were masterless *samurai* called *ronin.* By law ronin weren't allowed to carry a sword. So the shakuhachi was used not only as a musical instrument—if they left the heavy root on, it could also be used as a weapon."

"It doesn't sound very religious."

"Well, no, it doesn't, but at one time the Fuke sect attracted quite a few ronin into the fold. They joined because many of them, already acting as spies for the government, could, under the cover of monkhood, take advantage of the anonymity and unusual government privileges that this sect offered. These men were able to move freely about the country at a time when people weren't allowed to travel without special permits," Ozawa explained. "You see, Ray-san, the monks, wishing to remove themselves from worldliness, concealed their identity under rather strange-looking large, beehive-shaped hats called *tengai,* which were made from woven reeds. Each hat had only the smallest opening to see through. As I said before, the monks survived by wandering the country, playing shakuhachi for alms. It was the perfect disguise for these ronin spies."

"Are there any of these komuso monks in existence today?"

"Very few. You see, the Fuke sect that they belonged to was disbanded more than one hundred years ago. Since that time only a small number of dedicated monks have kept the tradition alive. As a matter of fact, for several years I was lucky enough to study with one of the few remaining komuso left in Japan."

"Is he still alive?" I asked.

"Yes, very much so. He's almost eighty-seven now. But unfortunately I wasn't able to continue studying with him because of my transfer to London, and now that I'm back I'm too busy with work." Ozawa gave an expression of genuine sadness. "I still see him occasionally, but these days I have little time for serious training. . . . I'm sorry, Ray-san. I'm talking too much." Ozawa seemed embarrassed that his self-discipline had slipped and revealed his true passion.

"No, please go on. I'm very interested, Ozawa-san." I had tried not to ask the inevitable question that my Western mind was begging to ask. Finally I succumbed. "How long does it take to become proficient in shakuhachi, Ozawa-san?"

Sucking air through his teeth, he thought about it for a moment and then replied, "It's case by case, Ray-san. It depends on how deeply a person wants to study shakuhachi. With the guidance of a good teacher, traditional Japanese folk music may take up to four years or more, but if you wanted to study the Zen classical pieces, it could be a lifetime pursuit, and you would need to study with a master player."

"Are there many teachers around now?" I asked.

"Quite a few actually, but really only a handful of great masters."

"Where would one buy a shakuhachi from—a maker or a teacher?"

15

"Traditionally, we'd buy it from our teacher, who, in turn, would buy it from his appointed maker. There are also a couple of shops in Tokyo that act as outlets for makers."

Ozawa then told me that, if I was interested in looking at some top-quality shakuhachi, one of the best places to visit was a shop called Mejiro, and that it was close to where I lived. I wrote down the address and said I was definitely interested in finding out more about this type of flute.

"Ray-san, it's 8:20. Our morning duties begin in ten minutes."

"Yes. Thank you, Ozawa-san. It was really interesting talking to you."

He took out his wallet and removed his name card from it. "Please call me in Tokyo if you have time. Perhaps we could meet again."

"Thank you," I said, and then realized I was still holding his flute in my hands. I passed it back to him, and we said good-bye.

Back at the dormitory, work groups were beginning their assigned tasks of polishing floors and performing general cleaning duties. My group was sent out into the brilliant morning light to sweep every inch of the temple grounds until each delicate blossom was captured.

Chapter Two
Pipe Dreams

After returning to Tokyo from the Zen retreat, I was only able to carry the stillness of the temple for a few days. During that time I wandered around in a sort of "Zen mental state," my back set straighter than usual, in a kind of affected "here and now-ness." For a while, I was in a "Now I'm filling the kettle, now I'm turning on the gas, now I'm striking the match" mode, but soon enough, the familiar racket of the city forced my senses to recoil and protectively suspend service. My new Zen philosophical tenet subsided, and, thankfully, my posture relaxed back into its old comfortable and familiar slouch. What did remain with me, though, were thoughts of that unusual Zen flute and those strange wandering komuso monks.

I told my wife, Dianne, in great detail, about my experiences at the temple, my meeting with the shakuhachi player, and the incredible pain of sitting in zazen. She made fun of the rigid way I now moved around the room, poking me in stiff areas of muscle that I didn't know I had.

"You don't need zazen, Ray; you need yoga! Why don't you start practicing with me sometimes? It'll really loosen you up and make you feel great, I promise."

"Yeah, I know. Maybe I will, but not yet. I'm too stiff."

Dianne and I had never been under any illusions about leaving our home near London to live in Tokyo. We knew it wasn't going to be all Zen gardens and tea ceremonies, and we weren't surprised when our feelings regularly fluctuated between finding the place fantastic and interesting and finding our stay pointless and terribly stressful. Japan is a country of extremes—to my mind, a country that frequently charms, yet at the same time baffles and sometimes even appalls. I was fascinated by this apparent dichotomy. There was, on the one hand, a majestic, Zen-like quality about the people, which constantly revealed itself through their daily actions. You could see it in their highly refined behavior, in their self-imposed discipline, and in their obsession with minute detail and perfection. These subtle qualities are, or more accurately this essence is, in everything from the ink stroke of a calligrapher's brush to the wrapping up of take-out sushi. It's everywhere and has evolved into an impressive social art form. Yet on the other hand, for all this sensitivity, the Japanese seem to have the ability to turn a blind eye, or more aptly a deaf ear, to aspects of their country that are out of control due to unrestrained materialism.

Commuting around Tokyo was nothing less than a relentless attack on the whole nervous system. We couldn't escape from the cacophony of sounds. Train stations blared out announcements every minute as trains rumbled to a halt, their warning signals nearly deafening. At forty-five–second intervals traffic lights played high-pitched, nauseating tunes as a cue to walk. And, as if the streets weren't crowded enough already, cyclists, not willing to use the busy roads, inched their way along the sidewalks, their brakes shrieking out an ear-splitting noise that made one want to commit a violent act every few seconds. When we asked the Japanese how they felt about these pressures, they'd simply answer, "*Shoganai*. Nothing can be done."

For the ten or more years that Dianne and I had already been together, we'd probably spent five of them overseas, exploring different parts of the world. Not content with three-week package holidays, the two of us would pack our bags and disappear for up to a year at a time. We were realistic people who knew how to adapt to most situations, however odd, and had enough experience to know how to cope with the ups and downs of living in a foreign country. In Japan, on low days, we reminded ourselves that we were here by choice and could leave at any time.

This wasn't our first stay in Japan. In the early 1980s we'd stopped over for five days on one of our trips to the Himalayas in northern India. Although our visit was brief, Japan had caught our attention, and we had filed away the possibility of living and working there in the future.

Japan was in the midst of a huge economic boom when we eventually did decide to move to Tokyo. There was euphoria in the air. Companies were investing in U.S. real estate at a staggering rate, and there was talk of the stock market reaching an all-time high. After years of hard work the Japanese people were finally enjoying a new level of disposable income. This new wealth was evident all around us.

Late-night trains were packed with inebriated office employees better known as *salarimen,* who were on their way home after a night out with their colleagues, courtesy of the company expense account. Wafts of *sake* fumes engulfed you as the doors of the train compartment slid open, and, filled with Dutch courage, these salarimen would muster the odd "Herro, how are you?"

Women wore the very latest in fashion. Designer labels, the trademark of success, were everywhere: on bags, hats, umbrellas, suits, ties. Every wrist seemed to have three months' salary strapped to it. I didn't have to read the financial papers to know how the economy was doing. I could gauge it by the piles of empty gift boxes, expensive liquor bottles, and shopping bags that were in the garbage each day. The "bubble economy," as it came to be called, was fully inflated.

Dianne and I soon set ourselves up amid the affluence and prosperity of Tokyo. Teaching jobs were plentiful, as English study was a fashionable hobby. In fact, it seemed as if language schools were opening up weekly to accommodate the masses. We were hired almost immediately.

Although there was much talk of internationalization in Japan, foreigners were still regarded with suspicion and kept at a safe distance outside of the teaching arena, so finding inexpensive accommodations wasn't as easy as finding employment. As non-Japanese we were encouraged to move into *gaijin* houses that catered to the "noisy, shoe-wearing-in-the-house barbarians." *Gaijin,* or literally "outside person," was the somewhat derogatory name given to all foreigners. Neither Dianne nor I particularly wanted to live in what was affectionately know as a "gaijin ghetto." We wanted a quiet place, somewhere where we could absorb a bit of the culture and get to know the people.

Dressed in our best clothes and with phrasebook in hand, we ventured out to the rental offices in the areas that we liked. At each stop we got the same negative reaction: either the arms crossed into an X sign meaning no, or the "gaijin, no" comment with the hand waving tightly under the nose.

Naively dismissing the possibility of discrimination, we pushed on, expanding our search to other neighborhoods. Still with no luck, we decided to phone some of the "for rent" numbers in the English newspaper. These people were more willing to deal with us, but most wanted to know what passports we held.

Some gaijin cause trouble, they'd say, adding that *some* gaijin "make noisy" and don't know when or how to put out the garbage.

Eventually, after much frustration and a taste of how hateful discrimination can be, we found a small *tatami,* or woven reed matting, room in an old two-story traditional-style wooden building. It must have been sixty or seventy years old and guaranteed to make you run for the door at the hint of a 2.4 on the Richter scale. There were six rooms, of which only three were occupied. The landlord, after showing us around, pointed to a large notice nailed to the outside of the building. It was an application for demolition and planning permission for a high-rise apartment block. He was patiently sitting on the property, waiting for land prices to reach an all-time high. Then he would sell. This year, next year—he didn't know exactly. We would be allowed to stay until they decided to pull the building down. Although Nature could serve us an eviction notice at any time.

Most Japanese didn't want to live in such old-fashioned places anymore. These buildings were symbols of the past and of poorer times. They were now only considered suitable for struggling students or misfits. From our point of view, such places were full of character, even charm, compared to the concrete jungle that was now Tokyo. For us it was a unique chance to live in an old-style Japanese house that within a few years wouldn't exist anymore.

We decided to live on the top floor closest to the fire exit, concluding that in the event of an earthquake, we'd have a better chance of surviving if we fell with the house instead of having it fall on us. Our room measured about eight feet by ten feet and included a kitchen nook with space for only one person at a time. We also had a gas outlet, a sink with cold water, and a cupboard for *futon* or mattress storage. If you were to spread your arms and spin, you could practically touch all the walls. At the end of the corridor was a shared squat toilet, and down the road was a public coin-op shower and a *sento,* which is a Japanese public bathhouse.

The problem of furnishing our new home was quickly solved. On a given day each week Japan's throw-away society was allowed to discard its unwanted household items. By simply walking around the neighborhood the night before garbage collection, we were able to find almost everything we needed. We brought home a refrigerator, a two-burner gas stove, shelves, a stereo, kitchen implements, and a small table—all in excellent condition.

Two weeks after my Zen retreat experience, Dianne arrived home and handed me a narrow box.

"Open it! Open it!" she yelled excitedly. "Hurry up!"

Inside the box was a navy blue corduroy bag containing a black plastic tube about one inch in diameter.

"It's a shakuhachi, Ray! What do you think? It's great, isn't it?"

"Yes," I said. "It's great." The only resemblance it bore to Ozawa's shakuhachi was that the bag was of similar design. "Where did you get it?"

She told me that, while walking round the Asakusa district with a Japanese friend, she passed an old man who was selling flutes at a street stall. The seller had, with great skill, demonstrated the instrument's capabilities. The plastic flutes, he'd told her, were for children to practice on, and at the low price of roughly twenty dollars, Dianne was sold.

Passing me a sheet of paper, Dianne said, "Look, he gave me this photocopy of the Japanese national anthem for you to practice."

There were no musical notes on the paper, just several columns of small circles that corresponded with the flute's five holes. By covering the blacked-out circles in each column on the flute, you could play the tune. It looked simple enough, which was just as well, because my musical experience was very limited.

For the next couple of weeks, when I wasn't teaching English, I practiced on my flute. I followed the dots and was surprised at how much I enjoyed blowing down my piece of plumber's pipe. Dianne, on the other hand, was regretting that she'd bought the damn thing. She was getting progressively more irritable with my toneless and hideously distorted interpretation of "Kimigayo" and by about the eighth day, she pointed out, in case I'd forgotten, that the two of us were sharing a one-room apartment not much bigger than a single garage.

"I can't handle it anymore!" she yelled. "The noise and repetitions are driving me crazy, Ray. You've got to start considering me, and for that matter, the poor bastard who lives in the next room! You'd go mad if someone was making that kind of noise around you all the time. You're going to have to try to limit your practice to times when I'm out from now on."

She was right. I'd become so preoccupied and engrossed in learning the piece of music that I'd neglected to realize how irritating and bloody awful it must have sounded. I wouldn't have put up with that noise for a minute.

Harmony was soon restored, and with a copy of Dianne's teaching schedule pinned to the wall, I carefully selected my practice times.

Within a few more days I was playing a rough but complete version of the Japanese national anthem. Spurred on by this small accomplishment, I decided it was time to visit the shakuhachi shop Ozawa had mentioned and look at some real flutes.

杉
風
之
調 Chapter Three
<u>Roots and Branches</u>

A rather exuberant woman shouted, "*Irasshaimase*. Welcome," as
Dianne and I entered. The interior of the shop gave off a woody,
musty aroma—a smell I liked instantly.

"Eh . . . may I help you?" she asked.

"Yes. Do you mind if we just look?" I asked, pointing to my eyes.

"Dozo. Please," she said.

The shop was stacked with bamboo shafts of various lengths,
all standing upright in large wooden tea chests, waiting to be made
into flutes. Shelves and boxes were cluttered with saws, reamers,
drills, and other paraphernalia needed to make shakuhachi. On
the counter lay a stack of sheet music and posters advertising
upcoming concerts. I noticed the beehive-shaped komuso hat on
display and wondered if it was for sale. And if so, who would
buy it? I carefully pulled one of the unfinished shafts out of its
box and inspected its unusual root on the end.

"Could I see some shakuhachi that have been finished?" I
asked, miming like a half-wit the action of playing a flute.

Dianne giggled at my stupid performance.

"Hai. Yes, of course." She unlocked a large metal filing
cabinet and slid open the top drawer. Using her hands, she

indicated that the lower drawers held longer flutes. There were six flutes in the top drawer, each one protected by a clear plastic bag.

"Dozo. Please. You try, please," the shop assistant said, passing me a flute she'd unwrapped. I placed it to my lips as Ozawa had shown me, and after several adjustments a low tone arose. It sounded nothing like the plumber's pipe. I heard a compassionate "Sugoi! Wonderful!" from the smiling women.

"Maybe you start beginner wood shakuhachi," she said, correctly appraising my level.

"Yes, may I see one?"

She walked over to a shelf, reached up, and took down a brown box. In it were the two parts of a wooden flute. She pushed the two halves together and handed it to me. It had been machine-turned on a lathe and looked much like a colonial chair leg. It had imitation bamboo nodes and a root, but it didn't have the ancient appeal of bamboo.

"Please you try," she insisted.

The same low tone struggled for life. I looked at the price—roughly two hundred and thirty dollars. Then I noticed that the bamboo flutes were priced from one thousand dollars up to six thousand dollars. I walked back to the wooden one, which now looked a little less like a chair leg.

"Maybe wood beginner one first," she suggested sensitively.

"Yes, good idea," I agreed happily.

"Bamboo shakuhachi very expensive," she said, reaching for a pencil and a piece of paper. She began writing first a one, then a long stream of zeros that totaled up to one million yen. And then she said, "Some shakuhachi," this time writing down two million yen. That equaled ten to twenty thousand dollars. *So much for a cheap hobby,* I thought.

Remembering that I would need some music to study, I asked about a book for beginners. She walked over to a shelf full of Japanese books and returned with a thin, green booklet that had several tunes written out in the same style as my photocopy of the national anthem.

I placed the money on a small money tray and handed it to her. She bowed, counted it efficiently, and then boxed and wrapped the wooden flute as if it was a priceless and rare object. While I waited, I looked through the small compact disc collection that was on display. The only one written in English featured an artist called Yokoyama Katsuya.

"Is this man a good player?" I asked.

"Sugoi, wonderful! Yokoyama Katsuya, *ichi-ban* — he number one player. Please," she quickly removed the same compact disc from her sample pile, convinced that we must hear it. Reverently she slipped the disc into the player and pressed play. I was overwhelmed at what I heard. The instrument had the power of a saxophone and yet the gentleness of a Western flute. The music soared and fell and went off into unfamiliar and unpredictable directions. It was the most sublime sound I'd ever heard. I wondered why I'd never heard this type of music before. The piece ended and the sales assistant, now looking extremely proud, said, "Yokoyama Katsuya, ichi-ban!"

"Ichi-ban," Dianne repeated in complete awe of what she'd just heard.

I removed the compact disc's insert and read the liner notes, which confirmed everything Ozawa had told me about the strange komuso monks. I was struck by a comment in the notes saying that the melodies reflected the true feelings of the wandering priests. I thought of other musicians I'd heard who had used their music to communicate the language of the soul.

John Coltrane's music had seized me in a similar way in a Soho record shop in London in the late 1960s. I asked the sales assistant what was playing.

"The best man . . . John Coltrane," he replied, handing me the record cover. The album was called *A Love Supreme*.

"I'll take it." I said.

"Good choice, man. . . . Coltrane's blowing the absolute truth," he said, capturing perfectly what I felt, but wasn't able to put into words.

The music I was listening to now was from a completely different genre than Coltrane's *Love Supreme,* but the similarities were striking. Each possessed exquisite tone color and perfect timing. There was that same intensity and seriousness, that same searching introspection. They were both "blowing Zen."

One week after I bought *A Love Supreme,* I was shopping for a tenor sax.

"Yokoyama Katsuya, ichi-ban," the shop assistant reminded me.

"I'll take it," I said.

I stole one last look at the bamboo shakuhachi. How could such a simple instrument make such extraordinary sounds? I was keen to get home and start practicing. As we left the store, the woman handed me a small package containing a cleaning rag for the flute.

"Service," she said, which is a word the Japanese use for a complimentary gift. She then bowed once, followed us out on to the street, bowed again, and waved until we were out of sight.

Now that I had my instrument, I had to find a place to practice where I wouldn't disturb anyone. Our room was obviously out of the question. The only place in the area with any kind of open space were the Arai Yakushi Temple grounds. Conveniently, this was only a five-minute walk from home. Wasting no time, I dashed over to the temple, flute in hand, to ask the head monk for his permission.

"Shakuhachi!" the monk exclaimed. "*Muzukashi.* Too much difficult."

Smiling with amazement, though, he consented and showed me an area where I could play. It was a perfect spot on the raised wooden verandah that surrounded the temple. The long, sloping roof would shelter me from sun and rain, and there was a peaceful view of the cemetery. The monk told me I shouldn't play after 9:30 PM each day or whenever the temple was being used for a ceremony or a festival.

Bowing slightly, he then said, "*Gambatte kudasai.*"

Gambatte, which means "to persevere, to never give up," is an important word in the Japanese psyche. Every individual, from kindergarten up, must be seen to make a strong effort towards their goal of success. Nothing is left to luck, and failure is unacceptable. If you ask the Japanese how they are, you will invariably hear "Very busy" or "Too busy." I once answered someone's casual inquiry with "Not so busy." "Oh, I'm sorry" was the response.

I bowed to the monk, agreed to study hard, and thanked him for allowing me to practice in his temple.

杉
風
之
調 <u>Chapter Four</u>
<u>Worlds Apart</u>

Every day for the next four weeks, when I wasn't working, I battled with my chair leg—I couldn't call it a shakuhachi yet! Changing from the low octave to the high octave seemed impossible. My lips trembled, and my fingers and wrists ached. I could only hold a sound for about five seconds. The more I tried, the more oxygen went to my brain. At times I became lightheaded and dizzy and had to sit down to prevent falling. I'd always thought that my lung capacity was fairly good, but now I had my doubts. I hoped it would grow stronger over time.

Slowly, I overcame the humbling and embarrassing feeling of muddling along, while strangers passing through the temple grounds watched and listened. Back home in London people would have thought it very strange to see someone practicing an instrument in such a public place. But because of cramped living conditions and paper-thin walls, music students in Japan had no choice but to practice in parking lots, parks, or tunnels. I would often see musicians gathered under bridges and in tunnels all over Tokyo. Many were professionals who said they couldn't afford the high cost of rehearsal rooms, and like me had to settle for an open-air studio.

After my first month of daily practice, my frustration finally peaked while standing in the temple grounds, and I was on the verge of hurling my "Zen weapon" into the abyss, alongside my sax from seventeen years earlier. I clearly needed a teacher. I searched through my wallet for Ozawa's card, and feeling very focused, walked to the nearest pay phone. His secretary said he was at a meeting and wouldn't be back until 2:00 PM. With two hours to wait, I returned to my spot at the temple and sat quietly on the verandah.

Why had something as simple as a bamboo flute, of all things, grabbed my attention? It had to be the challenge that was holding my interest because I certainly wasn't making any musical progress. Seven weeks ago I didn't know what a shakuhachi was. In the past, for one reason or another, I'd taken up all kinds of activities, always plunging myself into them one hundred percent. With most of these obsessions my motivation was always the end result, the glory, the success. I needed a goal, or what was the point? That was my attitude. I always turned everything into a race, a win-lose situation, and eventually, into something ugly and pressured. If I was going to pursue this new interest, then there was no way I wanted it to become a competition or a fixation. This was a chance to study the discipline of working at something every day without expecting instant gratification.

As I watched the temple scene around me, I wondered how long Dianne and I would stay in Japan. We hadn't given ourselves a time limit and had no expectations; we had simply agreed to let everything unfold. To know what we'd be doing a year from now was an absolute impossibility. Yet once there had been a time when I would have known exactly where I'd be and what I'd be doing.

Lying back with my hands behind my head, I stared up into the eaves of the overhanging roof, then closed my eyes.

Drifting off, thoughts of how I'd changed over the years and the internal struggles I'd gone through came to mind. . . . I had remained "emotionally bulletproof" until I was about twenty-seven years old. By the time I was twenty-one I was married and had a good job. Within a few years I bought a flat. Everything was great, and I moved steadily forward, not looking left or right. I worked hard and accumulated everything I wanted and needed to fit in. Having subconsciously learned at a young age to ignore any kind of emotional signals, I ended up getting a divorce by the time I was twenty-four.

Shaken, but not dramatically, I moved onward into greener pastures. Alone now, I faced time and space that needed to be filled. So without delay, I quickly buried any stray feelings of fear and hurt and plunged, headfirst, into the London nightclub scene. Within a short time I had a circle of friends who were looking for the same things—distractions, escapes, good times, and no grief. I felt comfortable with this lifestyle and at last I knew who I was:

Successful, outgoing, attractive, good prospect. Own flat in the city close to park and river, high-paid job with company car, vintage

Jaguar Mk.II, mint condition, vintage Triumph TR II being rebuilt. Martial artist, two top London nightclub memberships, Newcastle United supporter, quarter share in a racehorse.

That was my content.

Working from this identity I mostly got back what I put out. Image meeting image could be highly charged and exciting for a while, but really ugly when it started to break down, as it always did.

I kept up this frivolous lifestyle for a few years; then one day my bulletproofing started to fail me. In retrospect, this was inevitable. The mind can only take so much abuse; then it starts distorting and hungering for something more meaningful.

The first clue that something was out of balance came when I began catching revealing glimpses of myself and my friends. It was as if the regular cast in my head had gone on strike and decided to sit out the performance and watch. *Same script! Boring! Inauthentic!* they shouted.

I was beginning to realize my life was a sham, but I hadn't a clue what an "authentic" life was. How would I know authentic when I saw it?

I started seeing that there wasn't a shred of individuality among us. We'd become clones of one another. Our lives had been shaped by society, and by the culture we'd been brought up in. We never questioned it.

One night these unwanted feelings of dissociation became so strong that I had to leave a nightclub. I remember wading through the crowds in search of oxygen. Once outside, I began walking distractedly down Oxford Street. Walking always helped. Within forty-five minutes I reached Marble Arch, crossed Speakers Corner, and entered the blackness of Hyde Park. I headed through the trees, and after a few minutes came to a familiar open area. The last time I'd been here was seven long years ago, on July 5, 1969. There were thousands of people here that day. It was hot and I was sprawled out on the grass along with my fiancée. We'd all gathered to see the Rolling Stones. The concert was in memorial to the recently drowned Brian Jones. Mick Jagger, dressed all in white, read a poem called *Adonais* by Shelley and released thousands of white butterflies. It was a brilliant day.

Now, very much alone in the eerie darkness, I stood and listened to the distant sounds of the traffic speeding down Park Lane and looked out at the surrounding crown of city lights.

Seeing the shallowness of my life, I felt choked by sadness and an overwhelming feeling of loneliness. There had to be more.

I had no great epiphany that night. Only the overflowing of years of repressed feelings, dammed up behind what I now saw as an artificial existence.

Having spent years carefully filling every gap and hole in my life, I now found myself utterly and totally empty.

It was time for change, but change to what?

In the weeks and months that followed, my experience was intense and self-indulgent. I felt fearful and insecure and thought maybe I could cling to the old lifestyle, but adapt it somehow, make it more intelligent. Impossible—it was too late for that.

Soon I was off on a spiritual shopping spree, looking for answers in all manner of books. My choice of reading material bespoke my mind: shallow. I chose anything that offered a system or method, absorbing everything that suited me, and ignoring those ideas that didn't. It wasn't long before I realized that all I was doing was substituting one box of tricks and illusions for another, this time labeled "spiritual."

My friends didn't want to go anywhere near this stuff. Whenever I broached the "meaning of life" subject, they immediately barricaded themselves behind the most excellent English wit and humor. Some said the "transformation" was just a new way to add mystery to my personality, making me more attractive to women.

One night, a string of quips and jokes aimed at me and my "born-again bullocks" had us all rolling about on our barstools:

So Ray goes in search of this guru who lives on the top of the mountain. He climbs all the way to the top to ask what the meaning of life is. It takes him weeks to get to the summit. The guru's sitting there cross-legged, wrapped in rags. "Oh Great, but tattered, One, I have traveled for many days to ask but one question," gasps Ray.

"It is most gracious of you to be coming this far. Please be asking your question," says the Great One.

"What is the meaning of life, oh Master?"

"Life is a river, my dear seeker," the guru answers simply.

"Life is a river! Life is a bloody river! I've traveled all this way, and you tell me life is a bloody river?"

"Oh," says the guru. "Life is not a river?"

All their banter went along these lines. Then slowly, they realized I was serious. After that I became the boring bastard, the depressing navel contemplator. Who wanted to be around someone who thought he saw everything for what it really was? My telephone rang less and less. One of my closest friends did confide to me, in a moment of uncharacteristic honesty, that he often woke at 3:00 AM and had thoughts of the pointless way he was living. He said that the thought of stepping out of this lifestyle was as terrifying as falling into a dark bottomless pit. I said I thought it was the other way around—I felt I was stepping out of that pit.

I decided to move out of London and into the small town of Reigate in Surrey, which was about two hours south of the city.

The next year and a half was a real mixture of highs and lows. I felt bloody awful. I was discontented, full of disillusionment and insecurity. But at times I felt a real sense of clarity—even joy. It was in these clear moments that insights came, insights into the understanding of my environment and conditioning. I could see that I was always reacting based on compulsions and influences of my past. I was acting out of fear, determined by self-protectiveness and self-preservation. It wasn't long before I could watch these mind maneuvers without reacting to their demands. Clarity, at least for me, came by watching these games as they arose. There was a catch: It took energy and awareness. I cleaned up my diet and started eating more wholesome foods. I stopped drinking and started running. My health and energy level improved rapidly. There was nothing else I could do now except watch quietly and learn about myself without judgment.

These memories were interrupted by the sound of someone approaching. I opened my eyes and sat up. It was the head monk of the temple.

"Ah, Ray-san. You . . . no study today?"

"Hello, *Sensei,*" I replied, using the traditional title of respect for professionals. "I'm just taking a rest." I waited for one of his standard daily comments.

"Shakuhachi muzukashi. Very difficult," he said.

"Yes, Sensei. I know."

He went on his way, leaving me to the quiet surroundings. I looked at my watch. There was still one hour to wait before I called Ozawa again, so I lay back on the verandah and resumed my reverie.

I closed my eyes, and this time Dianne came to mind. The old London Ray would never have had a chance to get close to someone like Dianne.

I thought of our first meeting.

A friend had given me his ticket to an art exhibition and persuaded me to go in his place. He said the title of the show was "Man in Conflict." He gave me the catalogue a few days before the event. He had crossed out the word "Man" and replaced it with "Ray"! It made me laugh. I was still the brunt of friends' jokes, and although many parts of the old Ray were dropping away, I still had my sense of humor.

Interested in the exhibition, I decided it was worth the two-hour drive from my home to North London. The art show had the standard fashionable setup: glasses of champagne and wine, everybody well dressed, floating around, and admiring the pieces loudly. Within a few minutes an old friend spotted me, dashed over, and asked excitedly where the hell I'd been for the last year and a half. He had to go, but told me there was a party going on at Alan Matthews' place, and that I should get myself over there "pronto."

"Bring a bottle," he yelled as he made his exit.

Looking around to see if there was anyone else I knew, I noticed a very tall, attractive young woman talking with a group of people. They were standing in front of a very violent-looking abstract painting. For a second, I pictured the status that would be mine if I turned up at Alan's party with this woman. She had hair down to her waist and was casually, if a little untidily, dressed for the occasion. She had a vivacious energy about her and seemed totally at ease. I was immediately drawn to her and could feel the old Ray preparing to perform. As I attempted to join the group, the others started to move on, but she remained in front of the painting with another woman. Noticing me, she turned and smiled. I smiled back. Focusing my attention on the painting, I pretended, or at least tried to pretend, that I was interested in it. To my mind, it was crap. But if I was going to speak to her I would have to come up with something a bit more original than that.

Somehow sensing I was about to say something impressive, she turned to me and in the most perfect BBC English accent, said, "You're trying to think of something impressive to say, aren't you?"

39

I looked at her, my mouth gaping open for a moment. Then she and her friend broke the tension with laughter. At a loss for words, I was forced to tell the truth.

"Well, yes," I said with a laugh. "Actually, I was."

"It would be hard," she said, smiling.

"Yes, it's rubbish," I pronounced. *Why the bloody hell did I say that?* I thought.

"Quite," her friend said.

They moved on, and, feeling like a prat, I stared at the painting and decided it looked like a man with his head up his arse.

I made a complete round of the gallery, looking at one horrendous painting after another, soon coming to the satisfying conclusion that the painter was probably much more disturbed than I was.

The room was packed, and trays of food and wine were in abundance. I helped myself to a sandwich and a tomato juice, then made for a space near the door. Feeling a bit conspicuous, I considered having a glass of wine, but resisted. Searching the room, I spotted the beautiful woman with the long hair. She was at the buffet, emptying the contents of three or four vol-au-vents onto the serving tray, and refilling them with something else. She then proceeded to empty some sandwiches and fill them with some of the decorative vegetables and lettuce. This she did completely unselfconsciously. I started to smile, and, seeing that she had been caught in the act, she grinned back and then carried on with her restuffing.

With her plate overflowing, she came over and asked me if I would like to try a new and improved vol-au-vent. We introduced ourselves and talked and laughed easily. She bombarded me with bright, intelligent questions and was animated and funny, yet had a calm maturity about her. She gave me her fullest attention. As she was preparing to leave, I asked if we could meet again. She smiled and rattled off her phone number, then shook my hand and left. *A pen! A pen! Quick, I need a pen, please.*

Our first date wasn't in any of the wine bars or pubs I used to frequent. Instead, we took a walk, at Dianne's request, around a nearby lake.

After a great many walks around that lake and through the Surrey hills, we began to see each other on a regular basis. Those walks were the beginning of what would soon become a peripatetic lifestyle, with thousands of miles of walking and trekking with Dianne in various parts of the world, one of which was to be Japan.

Two rough-looking Japanese tomcats crawled out from under the temple verandah and crouched down a few feet from me. It was just after 1:00 PM, so the woman who regularly fed them would be along any minute. I glanced around the temple, looking at the places where I knew other cats would be hunched and waiting for a meal. They wouldn't come out until the woman was there to protect them from the two stocky thugs next to me.

"*Konichiwa.* Hello," she said when she finally came around the corner of the building.

"Konichiwa," I replied.

Cats raced towards us from all quarters, their stumpy Japanese tails upright. The woman made sure that the thugs were fed first, then started feeding the smaller, weaker cats.

Seeing me so often at the temple over the last month, she seemed to have adopted me along with the cats. She began to bring me homemade rice balls wrapped in *nori,* a light seaweed paper. I was always the last to be fed but never forgotten. I ate my rice balls and watched her fussing and scolding her feline friends. They didn't take much notice of her. They just wolfed down the rice.

"*Oishi.* Delicious," I said.

I was lucky today. She had put salmon in mine. Soon, pleased that she'd taken care of all of us, the woman took her leave.

At 2:00 PM I phoned Ozawa again. He was excited to hear from me, and quickly arranged for us to meet when he got off work that evening.

"Please meet me at Shinjuku Station at the west exit. Wait at the *koban,* the local police station, at 7:30 PM, Ray-san. I will find you."

杉
風
之
調 ## Chapter Five
A Corporate Warrior

Shinjuku is claimed to be the busiest station in the world, with more than 2.5 million people passing through it daily. I arrived early and entered the slow-moving stream of humans heading for the west exit. Everyone knew the rules. No one broke free of the flow to try to make it on his or her own. We were one perfectly synchronized and orderly group of people with no jostling or frustration. There was a certain beauty about being a part of it, yet not a part of it.

The ticket gate appeared without warning. I fumbled in every pocket for my ticket, and the ticket inspector was suddenly snapped out of the monotony of his job. I felt panic wash over me. As I looked back I saw hundreds of people waiting for me to move on, their journey timed to the exact minute. I apologized and was waved through by the white-gloved official. The commuters gushed through and hurried off to their evening destinations. Not wanting to look like I was trying to cheat the system, I waited and continued to search until I found my ticket, which I'd unconsciously folded into a minute square and placed in the top pocket of my shirt.

Handing over my now-unfolded ticket, I asked the inspector where I could find the police station. His hand indicated the direction. One of the commuters overheard and signaled me to keep in line and follow him. After about five minutes of wading slowly with the crowd, my guide's hand shot out and pointed to the right. I exited the mass of people and said, "Koban?" Another helpful hand pointed forward, and soon I arrived at the popular meeting place.

"Ray-san. Hello, how are you?" Ozawa was smiling.

He greeted me with the confidence of a long-time acquaintance, the camaraderie of the Zen retreat having made us feel like old friends.

"Ozawa-san. Hello. Have you been waiting long?"

After a series of tunnels, escalators, and elevators, we found ourselves in a restaurant on the fifty-second floor of a Shinjuku skyscraper. The decor of the place had the appearance of an airport lounge: air-conditioned with many chrome fittings, mirrors, and white walls. In fact, it had the ambiance of the inside of a huge refrigerator. Surely people only came here for the incredible view of the city and not for the atmosphere. The waitress showed us to our seats near the window, and with one skillful calligraphic zigzag movement, she wiped the table clean. Ozawa ordered beer.

As is the custom, he filled my glass, then I took the bottle and filled his. We toasted.

"*Kampai,*" I said.

"Cheers," he echoed.

"How's work, Ozawa-san?" I inquired.

Before answering, he removed a cigarette from its pack, lit it, then drew the smoke deep into his lungs.

"Too busy, I'm afraid, Ray-san."

I sympathized and asked him if he got much time off. Shaking his head, he went on to tell me about how he rarely had free time these days and seemed to be always under pressure. He said he missed the freedom of his life in London. He looked tired, and his face showed signs of stress. We talked about the retreat, and he said he wished he could visit there more often.

"I only get away from Tokyo four times a year. Twice to the Zen retreat, and twice to visit my old shakuhachi teacher. I sometimes wish I could give it all up and join a monastery," he said, half-joking, then added that life seemed only to consist of commerce and commuting these days.

I sensed he wanted to talk openly, so I willingly listened. He confided that since living in London he had found it hard readjusting to the Japanese system. He said he'd enjoyed working hard while overseas; he'd found it stimulating and rewarding. He'd enjoyed the frank relationships he'd had with his British coworkers and appreciated the private life he was allowed to have.

Back in the Tokyo office, he found the frenzied work pace to be unproductive and without substance. He complained of the psychological pressure that is heaped onto the workers at all levels. Ozawa mentioned that a colleague of his had recently died in tragic circumstances. At the end of the workday, he was found slumped in his seat on the Yamanote Line, which continuously circles the city. He hadn't arrived at work that day and had presumably died on the train at around 8:00 AM and had been riding the line ever since.

The sight of a salariman sleeping on the train is nothing out of the ordinary, Ozawa said. He added that he had no doubt that his colleague had died from overwork. The man was under a lot of pressure to keep up with his co-workers and increase the market share. Before he died he'd been working ten to twelve hours a day, plus commuting time and the obligatory after-work drinking sessions that were expected of him.

I felt saddened, even a little helpless, at not being able to suggest anything to relieve Ozawa's frustration. Fulfilling one's "duty" is so deeply ingrained in the Japanese that asking Ozawa to question what he was doing would be irresponsible and even dangerous.

Lightening up the conversation, Ozawa asked me about my life in London. I briefly told him of the work I had done as an electrical engineer, how I'd met Dianne, and the kind of lifestyle we had there. I stopped short of telling him how discontented I had once been and how that part of my life had gradually fallen away.

I quickly changed the subject and told him that I visited the Mejiro Shakuhachi Shop. His face lit up.

"*Honto?* Really?" he asked.

"Yes. The saleslady was really helpful. I bought a wooden shakuhachi and a compact disc by Yokoyama Katsuya," I said, hardly containing my excitement.

"Honto? Yokoyama Katsuya is one of the best players, Ray-san. Very powerful." He was soon lost in one of his favorite subjects. I talked about my daily practice and explained the difficulty I was having trying to learn the instrument on my own.

He told me of a retired colleague who taught a few private students, and said he would call to inquire about lessons.

After we left the restaurant for the station, we wandered above ground through a labyrinth of lanes and alleys. Buildings dazzled with colorful neon *kanji,* the Japanese characters, advertising stores' names and wares. I felt lucky that I couldn't read them—it would have taken some of the mystery away.

We strolled through the very heart of Shinjuku's pleasure district called Kabuki-cho, passing a Tudor-style coffee shop brightly lit and covered in plastic ivy. A giant crab with mechanical moving pincers tried to beckon us into its seafood restaurant. Speakers blared out high-pitched girls' voices from the doors of a fake Japanese medieval castle. The whole area was packed, noisy, and rowdy. Young girls dressed in miniskirts and high heels stood on the pavement handing out brochures.

We came to a large *pachinko* parlor. Pachinko is a pastime pursued by millions of Japanese. It's a game much like a vertical pinball machine, with a hand mechanism that controls a seemingly endless series of small steel balls. The glass doors to the parlor automatically slid open as we passed, letting loose the most terrific racket. It would be impossible to think in there. But maybe that was the point. Blank-faced devotees sat side by side, feeding the greedy machine small steel balls to win more steel balls to feed the machine. Perhaps these palaces were Japan's new zendos, or meditation halls.

When we made it to the station, we said our good-byes and thanked each other for an enjoyable evening. We promised to keep in touch.

Ozawa-san telephoned me three days after our meeting. He said he had called his retired colleague, Yamada-san, who was apparently willing to teach me the basics of shakuhachi playing. He said Yamada taught in Shinjuku and that I should telephone him to arrange my first lesson. And as if this favor wasn't enough, Ozawa then asked if I would like to meet his former sensei, the old komuso monk he had told me about. He was going to visit him on Sunday at his temple in Shimoda. Located on the Izu Peninsula, the small town of Shimoda is about three hours from Tokyo by train.

"Yes," I said. "I would be thrilled to go."

Chapter Six
An Old Soloist

The taxi driver told us that we were most fortunate, that our timing was perfect. He said that there'd been a continuous downpour for the last two days and that this was the first break in the weather the locals had had. Ozawa had managed to persuade him to take us to the front entrance of the temple, which meant driving his shining, white taxi three kilometers down a dirt road strewn with huge, muddy puddles.

Once off the main road, the scenery became almost timeless. Somehow this small area had been spared the controlling concrete and tarmac that smothered most of Japan. We passed several old farmhouses, their distinctive high-pitched thatched roofs dilapidated and filled with moss and wild growth. Most, understandably, had been abandoned by a new generation of farmers who favored the modern, convenient, cement boxes that characterized Japan's architecture these days. Even through the decay, I could see that the old houses were still full of character and beauty. Their forlorn presence portrayed a rapidly vanishing Japan that could never be retrieved.

The dirt road wound slowly on through the countryside, passing drenched rice paddies on all sides. I could see the seedlings, still young and pale green in color. The farther away we got from the main road, the farther we seemed to be traveling back in time.

Our driver, a chatty, round-faced man with tightly permed hair, pointed proudly with a white-gloved hand to one open area, explaining that it once belonged to his family. He said they had lived in Shimoda and worked as rice farmers for four generations. When his father died, his older brother refused to take over the land, saying that he had made a better life for himself in the city. So, the remaining family agreed to sell.

Through Ozawa, he asked me what my ancestors had done. His question was asked casually, the way most people would ask, "What does your father do?" I thought for a moment, then explained that my father had been a shipbuilder and my grandfather a coal miner, both in the North East of England. Beyond that, I didn't know.

His head nodded slowly, and he sucked air between his teeth to show his admiration and respect, saying, "Very difficult work."

I agreed. He wanted to know if I had followed in my father's footsteps. I told him I hadn't, but had chosen to go south to London to find less grueling employment and greater opportunity. He tutted, nodded his head again slowly, and said that he understood.

"So you're here on business in Tokyo?" he asked inquisitively.

"No, at the moment I'm living here temporarily and working as an English teacher," I said.

I returned the conversation to the subject of rice and asked when these fields would be ready for harvesting. He said in early

November, and went on to say that the emperor and the nation would be able to taste the country's first harvest of the year at that time. His mention of the emperor in connection to rice surprised me.

Later, I realized that Japan, like so many other Asian countries, considers rice to be deeply sacred. The people depend on it both spiritually and physically. Even amid the high technology and fast pace of modern Japan, every phase of its cultivation is religiously sanctified. Every February, before the rice has been sown, the emperor, once considered a living deity, presides over an ancient ritual within the Imperial Palace shrine. It's his duty to implore the gods to bestow a blessing on the rice farmers. In the spring the farmers participate in a seedling planting ceremony, then in the autumn, if the gods have been generous with rainfall and sunshine, there are two more important events. One in mid-October, when the rice is taken from the first crop and offered to the gods in thanks, and then, as the driver mentioned, in November, when the emperor and the people taste the first harvested rice of the year.

This drive through the countryside was a real pleasure, allowing me to look far into the unobstructed distance, something I couldn't do in Tokyo. Rounding a bend in the road, I could see the small temple of Ozawa's sensei, set at the foot of green rolling hills.

The taxi driver, upon arrival, uncharacteristically climbed out of the car and shook our hands before saying good-bye and driving off. I wondered if he would take the rest of the day off to wash his car.

Ozawa and I climbed up some crude stone steps and, passing under the rough wooden *torii* gate, symbolically left the secular world behind.

"Maybe there will be more rain?" Ozawa said absently.

To the south, dark clouds were crowding, accented by a silver sky. Everything felt closer on days like this—nature's sounds more amplified in the stillness, a stillness one feels deep within a forest. Trees and plants had been washed clean by the rain, the wetness deepening the colors. Warmth drew the moisture from the ground, and a faint mist hung in the air.

There was a cluster of simple, unpainted buildings up ahead. Their appearance created an atmosphere of extraordinary calm and gave the impression that they could be uninhabited. Nothing stirred.

"*Gomen kudasai.* May we come in please?" Ozawa called out. Seconds later an apologetic elderly woman, wearing a simple brown kimono and wraparound apron, arrived and carefully opened the wooden sliding door.

"Ozawa-san. *Ohisashiburi desu ne!* Long time no see!" Ozawa introduced me.

"Dozo, dozo," she beckoned with her hand to come in, come in please. "I'll make tea," she said, smiling openly at both of us.

As is the custom, our shoes were efficiently replaced with guest slippers, and we were ushered into a tatami-mat room. Quickly the frosted-glass sliding doors were opened, giving us a view of a small, sheltered, mossy Japanese garden, its beauty subtle and unpretentious. The scent of rain-soaked earth drifted into the room. Then, with more delightful apologies, the housekeeper backed out onto the verandah and disappeared.

There was a deep silence in the room, caused by the thick matting and sparseness of decoration. We sat quietly, and I took in my surroundings.

The room was of medium size and had an unsophisticated alcove over on one side. In the alcove was a faded *sumi-e* style wall hanging, its black-and-white brush strokes creating a rocky waterfall with an old sagelike figure standing below it, leaning on a tall stick. Beneath the hanging was a delicate arrangement of flowers. The matting covering the floor gave off a pleasant aroma of straw. It looked old and had lost its shine. The walls were finished with some sort of fine, gritty sand-colored paint, and between each panel was a dark strip of wood. The sliding doors were the only source of light in the room, apart from a circle of fluorescent lighting above us. The only piece of furniture in the room was a low square table, at which we were now kneeling.

Hearing the sound of the sliding door opening, I looked up to find that the person entering the room wasn't the frail and wizened old monk that my mind had conjured up, but instead a rather hale-looking, sprightly man. Ignoring his gestures to stay seated, Ozawa and I both stood up and bowed politely, Ozawa much more deeply than I. I was introduced to and warmly greeted by the old monk. His name was Teruhiko Ota, but Ozawa simply called him Sensei. He gratefully accepted our gifts of fruit and rice crackers.

A few moments later the housekeeper entered again, carrying a rustic-looking teapot and three large cups. She poured the tea carefully, explaining to me that it was *ban-cha,* which is a rough grade of Japanese tea with less caffeine then the refined green tea.

"Vely hellcee," she said shyly in English. The old monk said something in jest to her, and she affectionately scolded him before leaving the room.

Once the formalities were completed, Ozawa and the monk cheerfully exchanged news for a few minutes. As they talked together, I could see the respect and affection my friend had for this aged man. The old monk sat gracefully; his posture strong and upright, he seemed almost rooted to the floor. His voice was soft, his tones warm and relaxed. I felt at ease and sat quietly, sipping the earthy-tasting tea.

On the train journey down, Ozawa had talked a little about Ota Sensei and told of how the old monk had tragically lost both his parents in the 1923 Kanto earthquake. He was twenty-two years old at the time. The loss was a crushing, confusing, and isolating experience for him.

His father had been a carpenter by trade, and had trained his son in the same profession from as early as the time that he could hold a tool. They were very close. Whenever they had spare time, the young Teruhiko diligently studied shakuhachi with his father, also learning to make the rough unlacquered flutes in the family workshop.

Because Tokyo was virtually destroyed by the quake, the government appealed to the nation to help build shelters for the homeless. People with any kind of building skills were in great demand and were asked to share their knowledge and teach others. For the next two years, young Teruhiko Ota built houses and more or less lived from hand-to-mouth like so many others at that time. Then one day he found himself working in one of the temples that had been partially destroyed. In exchange for work, he was given board and lodging. Apparently he easily adjusted to the temple environment, and for the first time since the disaster, started examining the great sorrow that was left inside him. For solace, he resumed his music practice, and in between work, began showing one of the younger monks how to play shakuhachi. It was during this time that he became interested in the almost extinct komuso tradition of suizen, and started to understand its Zen connections more deeply.

With the completion of his work at the temple, Ota decided to go to a monastery in Kyoto to study Renzai Zen. Renzai Zen emphasizes vigorous training, including the study of *koans,* or paradoxical dialogues, which are intended to break through the limitations of the ego and point to the true self. Two of the most common koans being: "What is the sound of one hand clapping?" and "Does a dog have Buddha nature?"

With each year of study, Teruhiko moved farther away from the secular world and more and more into the world of Buddhism. Eventually, he received monastic ordination, but feeling no connection to the ritualized ceremonies, he decided to leave the monastery and devote himself to meditation through shakuhachi.

He told Ozawa that he would often play for hours by the roadside on the way to a temple, losing himself in the purity of sound.

I had been studying Japanese every spare moment since my arrival in Japan and knew enough of the language that I managed to pick up the gist of their conversation as it turned more serious. Ozawa was apparently apologizing and telling the monk how he didn't have time to study shakuhachi because of the demands of work. The old monk listened and nodded, sympathetically, then said that he worried that Ozawa was damaging his health with too much work in the city.

Their conversation ended, and we quietly sipped our tea and rested our eyes on the lovely scene through the open doors. The long, relaxing silence ended when the monk, looking directly at me, softly began to speak in Japanese. Ozawa expertly translated.

"Ozawa-san has told me a little about you. He said you came from London and have been living in Japan for several months."

"Yes, I'm here with my wife."

"Is this your first visit?"

"No, it's our second; we were here a few years ago but only for five days."

The old monk, having a momentary lapse of memory, asked Ozawa if we met in London.

"No, Sensei. We only met a few weeks ago. We were both at a Zen retreat near Shimoda."

"*Ah, so desu ne, so desu ne.* I see, I see. Had you studied Zen before that, Ray-san?"

"Not specifically, although I have read quite a bit about it. To be honest with you, my participation in the Zen retreat was more as a tourist than as a practitioner."

This comment seemed to greatly amuse the monk. He burst out laughing.

"Zen tourist. Zen tourist," the monk repeated several times, laughing loudly at my choice of words. Ozawa and I joined in, seeing the funny side of my comment.

"There is some interest about Zen in the West, isn't that so, Ray-san?"

"Yes, Sensei, there are quite a few people interested in a Zen approach to living. The word seems to be popping up everywhere these days. There are many Zen-themed books written in English."

"Yes, I have heard this." He sighed. "Zen is just another word for living everyday life in this moment. Of course, the physical body is living in the moment, but mentally there's very little awareness of this. The mind is so cluttered and always wants to be somewhere better, always traveling into the past or future. Always comparing." He paused to sip some tea, then said, "If the mind is clear, it acts like a mirror and gives an immediate and undistorted view of the world and not an interpretation. It's simple really, Ray-san, so simple that I think it would be difficult to fill a whole book about it." He chuckled and then continued talking. "Seeing and dealing with things as they are—that's all."

"Ozawa-san said you are also interested in shakuhachi."

"Yes, I am, Sensei. As a matter of fact, it's because of the flute that Ozawa-san and I became friends. I overheard him playing in a garden, and I was unable to resist the sound, so I followed it."

"Did you know the shakuhachi before that?" he asked.

"No, not really. I think I might have heard its sound mixed into some Western music once, but I never knew the name of the instrument or how it should really sound."

As Ozawa translated my last comment, he started laughing and said in English and Japanese, to both of us, that he didn't think his playing these days was a good representation of "how it should really sound."

"He is a fine player, Ray-san, but he works too hard in that foolish office of his, so he has no time to keep up with his practice."

Smiling, Ozawa crouched down with his hands protecting his head in mock submission. His teacher laughed and wagged a finger at him. A tangible affection flowed between them.

I told the old monk that I had bought a wooden shakuhachi for beginners and that Ozawa had found me a teacher in the Tokyo area.

"Ah, so desu ne! I see," he said.

"Yes. I'm looking forward to having some instruction. It's been difficult studying without a teacher," I said.

"Yes. Studying alone would be difficult and could cause a great deal of frustration, Ray-san. Shakuhachi is not really an instrument that one can take up casually just for entertainment. It takes infinite patience and great presence of mind to learn it. If played with passion and without motive, it can become much more than just a musical instrument. For me, it's been a valuable tool that has helped to unfold the deeper, more important questions of life. It's been a fine teacher, and many times the harshest of mirrors," he added, laughing loudly again. "As you study, don't be concerned about 'Am I getting better?' Just practice for its own sake, and let progress take care of itself. Don't corrupt the beauty of learning by becoming attached to an end goal."

I nodded, indicating that I understood his words, and thanked him for his advice.

Curious to hear about his life as a komuso, I broached the subject and asked him to tell me a little about his time as a wandering monk.

In an open and easy way he reiterated some of what Ozawa had told me—how he studied Zen as a young man and how he left the monastery to walk the length and breadth of Japan. He said he roamed, in all weathers, from temple to temple playing shakuhachi by the side of the road as he went. When he was hungry, he placed his donation box around his neck and his begging bowl on the ground and played meditation pieces. In return, people gave him food and sometimes money.

"You must have spent a great deal of time in solitude, Sensei," I commented.

"Yes. For weeks at a time I didn't speak to anyone, not even in the temples. Most of the time I was immersed in my meditations and completely alone. I became very sensitive to everything around me—the animals, the birds, the plants, the trees. They all became a part of me. There were times, though, when there was separation from nature. The birds were silent and the trees and plants were indifferent, and I was overcome with an aching lone-liness, lost in my own thoughts. Other days I blew shakuhachi for hours in total abandonment of the self. It was an innocent time; I belonged to nobody," he said.

"How long have you lived at this temple?" I asked, wanting to know when he ceased his mendicant lifestyle.

"For many, many years now. I can hardly remember. But I do remember only meaning to stay for a week." More laughter.

Ozawa, offering more information, said, "It was more than thirty years ago when Sensei arrived here, Ray-san. The temple had been completely neglected during and after the Second World War and was badly in need of repair, so he stayed on and helped to raise much-needed money. Teaching shakuhachi was one of the ways he could help. Many students came, and soon it became a place for serious study and practice." He turned to Ota Sensei and briefly translated what he was saying and then resumed his conversation with me.

"When enough money was collected from the locals, and with the earnings from the students, Sensei supervised the rebuilding of the temple. I was only about fifteen years old at the time, and actually became part of the group that helped."

The old monk joined in the conversation again.

"There was much dedication from the pupils, and no need for me to move on. I am the last remaining monk here now. The local people from the village show great kindness and regu-larly come to visit me and make sure I'm behaving myself." He chuckled fondly.

I wanted him to go on talking about his life as a komuso, but he decided to change the subject and find out more about me, asking several questions about England and the Iron Lady, Prime Minister Thatcher. He marveled that a woman had become so successful in such a predominantly male business. He said he wished that it could be so in Japan. He then went on to ask me about my impressions of Japan, so I gave him my well-rehearsed and tactful responses along the lines of: The people are very polite; the cities are very safe; the culture is very interesting. . . .

"Umm, Umm, Umm," he responded impatiently as I spoke. I could tell he was losing interest in my inane answers by the way he abruptly cut me off in midsentence.

"Sensei wants to know if there's *anything* that you find disappointing here, Ray-san? There's no need to hold back; he would rather hear your frank observations, if you don't mind," Ozawa said.

I was surprised by his request and hesitated for a moment, trying to think of something disappointing but not too disparaging.

"Well, Sensei, before I came to Japan, I'd known that the environment had suffered due to rapid economic growth. But when I actually arrived and traveled around, I was quite shocked at the true extent of the destruction. There are only small pockets left of what must have been a very beautiful country once. What's more alarming is that the people don't seem to see it," I said.

Ozawa and the monk, looking serious, nodded at my comments. Drawing in a deep breath, the monk started speaking.

"It's true, it's true, Ray-san. Forty years, that's all it took to destroy it all. Without any questions asked, we gave it all up. For what? Now it's too late. It's all gone. The people don't see it because they're too busy seeking success. And what has this madness brought us? Full pockets and empty hearts. Work. Work. Work. No relationship with anything, only work. You read of people dropping down dead on the job from being overworked," he concluded.

Ozawa, remembering our conversation from the other night, gave me a knowing look. We all sat quietly, as if giving a minute's silence to the passing of Japan's once-great beauty.

Ozawa broke the silence and said in English that these were subjects that his teacher felt strongly about and discussed frequently when they met. After a short pause, the monk started up again, this time with only a short burst of words. Ozawa didn't quite understand what the monk was saying. I waited while he furiously skimmed through his Japanese-English dictionary, apologizing as he did so, for forgetting the word.

"Fury? Violence? No, that's not quite it." He thought about one of the words the monk had said, drawing the Japanese character on his left hand with his finger.

"Maniacal. Maniacal employees," he said. "Sensei wants to know what you think about Japanese workers and the way they live their lives."

It was uncommon for the Japanese to be so direct.

"That's a difficult question, Sensei. We all carry the weight of our cultural conditioning," I said. I was hedging because I knew this subject was a painfully sensitive one for Ozawa.

"Yes, yes, Ray-san. But is it a meaningful existence? Is it a true way of living?" He seemed to want to pin me down.

"It would be presumptuous of me to make a comment about what a meaningful existence is or what is true for someone else, Sensei. I can only speak from my own experience."

"You're quite right, Ray-san," replied the monk.

"For me," I continued, "it would be foolish to work to the point of making myself sick at the expense of all my relationships."

"Yes, but what would you say was a meaningful life, Ray-san?" Ozawa asked me in English. The monk nodded to show that he understood what was said.

"Well, I would say that . . . first it's important to see how we are *really* living in our daily lives. Unless we see this clearly, then the question is only speculative and without any meaning. What I mean by clearly is that we have a direct understanding of why we are living the way we are, without any distortion."

The monk excitedly joined in.

"I have heard much about psychologists and the self-improvement movement in the West," he said.

I quickly interrupted him in midsentence, perhaps too quickly, giving away a prejudice against both ideas. "The direct understanding I'm talking about, Sensei, doesn't need the guidance of a psychologist, or some future ideal of self-improvement," I said respectfully.

"Yes, Ray-san. I was just about to say that understanding is an entirely different matter," he said. "It's more important to look and clear away what isn't true or meaningful rather than spend a lifetime searching for what is true and meaningful. This means clearing away all the rubbish and accepting without any distortion the nature of who we really are and not who we think we are." He paused for a moment, then said, "See what you're left with after you've cleared away what isn't meaningful. This takes a great deal of energy."

We sat contemplating the words, and then the monk spoke again.

"Many people pass through here. All are trying to find solutions to their problems and make some sense of the world. Their minds are jumbled with beliefs, ideas, and delusions. They come here to meditate for hours on end. They say it gives them peace of mind," he said. " 'Go home and find out why you have no peace with anything around you,' I tell them. 'If your relationships in your daily life are false, you can come and meditate until you get calluses on your backside, but your relationships in daily life will still be false.' They don't like to hear it, Ray-san. They don't like it that I speak my mind to them. They complain that I'm rude and unkind, ha! They don't come back. They don't really want to know. They use the great beauty of meditation as an escape. Zen tourists, Ray-san."

I smiled and nodded in agreement, and remembered a time when I had been paralyzed by the search for solutions.

Starting to feel concerned for Ozawa, who had been translating now for over an hour, I paused, and at that moment, the housekeeper appeared on the verandah with a fresh pot of tea. The distraction was timely and grounded us pleasantly. I asked Ozawa if he was tired from translating for so long, and he assured me that he was fine and was enjoying the conversation very much. As we sipped our fresh tea, he said he was pleased to see his teacher so lively.

The old monk reached across the table and held my hand. The simplicity of the gesture made any feeling of separateness drop away.

"Ray-san, if you decide to study shakuhachi seriously, you will find that as your practice deepens there may be moments of liberation. Don't attach yourself to such fleeting trivialities. Liberation is not the goal. Liberation is the practice in this moment; it's in everything we do."

It started to rain outside, the noise suddenly filling my ears.

Ozawa and the monk began speaking again. I heard the word shakuhachi as they conversed with each other.

"Sensei would like to play a piece for us, Ray-san."

"Really? *Domo arigato gozaimasu.* Thank you very much, Sensei."

The monk excused himself and then returned carrying a very long bamboo flute, perhaps thirty inches in length. It was about half as long as he was tall. He walked to the corner of the room, knelt carefully, and sat in the *seiza* position, with his legs folded under him. Unceremoniously, he placed the flute to his lips. The bulky root end almost touched the floor. With his thumb covering the hole in the back, his fingers stretched as far as they could to cover the four holes on the front. Composing himself, he began. His lower abdomen moved slowly in and out, resting before inhaling. Each long phrase was played in one breath. His head moved from side to side, subtly altering the rich tones, fingers moving along the shaft, sometimes fully covering the holes, sometimes half-covering them.

He made the bamboo come alive, capturing the sounds of the universe and bringing them into the room. Long, deep, haunting tones vibrated in my chest. The notes demanded introspection. The noise of the rain somehow accentuated the silence between each phrase, adding an inconceivable dimension to the music.

Any expression after the music ended would have been depreciatory. This wasn't a performance. The monk placed the flute on the floor in front of himself, uttered a word Ozawa didn't translate, then went on to explain what he played.

"That was an original komuso piece, or *honkyoku,* as we say in Japanese. It's called 'Ajikan,'" he said.

Ozawa translated the title to "All Is Emptiness—Emptiness Is Form." The monk went on to say that without discipline and a serious mind, it is impossible to achieve mastery of the shakuhachi. A true master plays from emptiness, creating form.

"Zen honkyoku pieces, Ray-san, are just music until you master them. Then they become suizen."

Suizen. I remembered that this is what Ozawa had called "blowing Zen."

The monk rose to his feet and walked back to the table. Ozawa and I bowed in thanks.

"Learn to listen with your whole being, Ray-san. Listening is the gateway to liberation."

The rain stopped, and I asked if it would be all right to take a walk around the garden. I needed air and wanted to give Ozawa a chance to spend some time alone with his teacher.

After thirty minutes, they joined me in the garden. Our taxi was here. It was time to leave. We thanked the monk for his hospitality and said our good-byes.

"Please come back and visit again, Ray-san."

I thanked him and said I would. As we pulled away, he and the housekeeper waved farewell.

Chapter Seven
A Tale of Two Teachers

I stepped out into the intense humid heat of an August afternoon on my way to my first shakuhachi lesson. Within minutes of leaving my apartment, the sweat was running down the inside of my trousers, and my shirt was sticking to my back. There wouldn't be any relief until I hit the cover of the air-conditioned shopping arcade that led to the station. Avoiding the main road with all its noise and fumes, I walked down the narrow back streets, occasionally stopping to let a car or truck squeeze past me.

I amused myself with the thought that it must be against the law in this city to leave a tree standing. It would give shade, and people would gather there. It would hold up the traffic!

During the unbearably hot summer months, Dianne and I were rising at 5:00 AM most days to take advantage of the cool early mornings.

We'd jog to the little cement park and circle the baseball diamond a few times, do some stretching, then sit on a bench next to an artificial waterfall and watch the other joggers and people pass by with their dogs.

I was distracted on this particular morning and started telling Dianne that I wasn't sure about what I was getting myself into with the shakuhachi.

"What's the problem?" she said, seeing that I was serious.

"I'm concerned that it will take up too much of my time. It's already taking up quite a bit now."

"If you're enjoying it, Ray, carry on. Don't question it. If you're worried about me, don't be. I'll tell you soon enough if it gets in the way of us. You haven't even had your first lesson yet, and already you're anticipating tomorrow. Just flow with it, Ray. See where it takes you."

I was the one who always talked of nonattachment. Dianne was the one who practiced it.

"Yes. But what if I really like it, then we want to leave?"

"I can't answer that question, Ray. Why don't you have your first lesson before you think about giving something up you've barely started?"

The shopping arcade was packed with browsers seeking shelter from the heat. I stopped off and bought a can of juice with the unappetizing name of Calpis. Farther down the arcade, I bought a box of spongy, sweet-bean cakes for my new teacher.

When I arrived at the studio, I knocked on the metal door and heard a barely audible voice that I took as a signal to enter. Two people, both holding flutes, sat in the center of the large room in seiza, facing each other. My first reaction was one of despair. There was no way I could carry out the lesson in the kneeling position. It crossed my mind that I should start limping and tell them I had a knee problem.

"Ah! Ray-san, please, please come in. I am Yamada. You'll find some slippers there. We are just finishing."

With that, the teacher said something to his student, who quickly collected his music sheets together and started to dismantle his flute.

"No, no. Please don't stop, Sensei," I protested. "My lesson isn't until three o'clock."

I'd deliberately come early in the hope of perhaps hearing one of his students play. The student, a young man, poured us each a glass of iced tea and then sat at the side of the room.

Ahhh, not fair, I thought. *He's going to stay and listen to me play.* I felt a strong urge to tell him that I was a beginner, but I managed to stop myself.

"This is Ray-san's first lesson," Yamada informed his student, bringing me some relief.

"Honto," he said, seeming a little disappointed and less interested in sticking around.

"Please," Yamada said, shaking my hand in a welcoming gesture. "Relax and cool off for a moment. There's no rush."

I drained the glass and wiped my face and hands with a cloth, then went over to sit on the floor in front of my new teacher. He said that the lessons were sometimes long and asked if I would prefer to sit on a chair. Gratefully, I agreed, and the student brought one over for me. Now, I was looking down on Yamada, who sat comfortably cross-legged on the floor.

We talked for a few minutes and then, both eager to get started, began the lesson. He asked me to blow a series of notes and, as I did this, he moved closer and quickly corrected my mouth position and the angle of the flute. Noting my posture, he told me to sit up straight, then began demonstrating the same series of notes, now asking me to follow. Guidance at last! He cheered at the progress I'd made on my own and encouragingly told me that I had good pitch.

After hearing a few of my dismal notes, the student excused himself. The atmosphere became relaxed, and, during the course of the lesson, every so often, Yamada would stop teaching and begin to chat about something totally unrelated to shakuhachi. Soon I learned that this was his style, and there wasn't any set time for the lesson to end.

I had assumed the residential address that I had been given was Yamada's home. But when I arrived, I was surprised to find that it was in fact a large shakuhachi studio that he had set up in an apartment building. His home, he told me, was outside the city and more than an hour and a half away by train. The place was primarily for shakuhachi students, whom he taught between the hours of noon and 7:00 PM, Monday through Friday. Students were charged a modest monthly fee, which allowed them to drop in any number of times within that month. At the end of the lesson, as I was preparing to go, Yamada said, "Please come to the studio anytime, Ray-san. Every day if you wish."

Working in the district of Shinjuku and living in Nakano, which was only one stop away on the Chuo train line, meant it was easy for me to drop into the studio most afternoons. Yamada was delighted with my regular attendance, and as time passed, we slowly got to know each other. I learned that he had been retired from corporate life for four years, and had since endeavored to immerse himself in his lifelong dream of being a shakuhachi teacher.

He said he'd joined his company when he was only nineteen years old and had given them unquestioning loyalty until his retirement day. As he talked, I thought of Ozawa and calculated that he had at least another twenty-five years left of his sentence. Yamada confessed that his work had been his sole identity for more than forty years. Shaking his head gently, he told me how he had caught the 7:28 AM train every day for most of his working life. He added almost wistfully that he'd seen many of the same people in the same carriage for all those years, yet had never really spoken to any of them.

Typically, his job came first and his family second, so he'd had little spare time for outside interests. As a student, he'd wanted to become a professional shakuhachi player and teacher, but his father, believing it would be impossible to make a proper living with the shakuhachi, told him his goal was foolish and unrealistic. With Japan still reeling from its defeat in World War II, Yamada had reluctantly joined the work force and accepted the fact that the shakuhachi could never be anything more than a hobby for him.

When the average salariman, or office worker, retires in Japan, he has to reenter a foreign world. Every part of his life has been devoted to the company: his identity, his friends, all his worth.

Nothing else really matters as long as he is accepted by his company and colleagues. Upon retirement, these office workers are suddenly abandoned and are often ill equipped to cope with having free time and a life of their own. Many go home to a wife they hardly know, in a house they've only really slept in for forty years. Having had no time to develop hobbies, outside friends, or interests, many soon experience acute identity distress and depression.

This, happily, was definitely not the case for Yamada. By setting up his studio, he had secured for himself a full and busy retirement.

Yamada's philanthropy amazed me, and I often wondered how he could afford to run this studio in one of the most expensive districts in the world. My questions were soon answered by one of his regular students. He said that when Yamada retired, he and some other individuals started up the studio with the financial backing of a wealthy industrialist. In the beginning, it was more than a shakuhachi studio. They put on special cultural events, hiring different teachers to instruct classes in tea ceremony, flower arrangement, Japanese cooking, and many other arts.

For three years it was a place where both Japanese and foreigners came together to experience the Japanese arts. Then one day, due to financial pressures, the industrialist was forced to withdraw his support. Yamada, not willing to give up on his dream, decided to stay on and finance the studio himself by taking out a loan secured on his land in the countryside.

Currently, he was paying all the bills but still insisted on only charging the small monthly tuition fees. He seemed to be realizing his dream at a terrific price.

My first few weeks of lessons consisted mostly of trying to hold each note for as long as I could. At first this was only for five or six seconds at a time. Yamada also taught me a series of finger drills that eventually turned into simple Japanese nursery rhymes. I'm sure these were painful to the ear, but he encouraged me constantly and told me that even if it seemed impossible, to keep trying regardless. He assured me that with enough diligence and practice, all obstacles would be overcome.

Yamada's enthusiasm for teaching was evident by the huge amounts of energy he put into each lesson. Sometimes our sessions, which were meant to be an hour long, lasted for two or three hours at a time. My wrists and fingers ached from holding the flute for so long, and for several days I had to stop playing because I had developed tendinitis in my right wrist.

Over several months I learned to read and sing Japanese music, and began to appreciate the finer, more subtle points of the flute. I soon progressed from nursery rhymes to folk pieces, and then Yamada said I was ready for the famous classical composition "Rokudan." It was a difficult piece that was written in six sections and lasted an incredible twelve minutes. Under the constant guidance of Yamada, I slowly and agonizingly worked my way through it. In the traditional Japanese way of teaching, he played along with me, setting and resetting the tempo and pitch each time I wandered off.

Yamada sometimes offered a glass of sake to his students before starting a lesson.

"It will loosen you up," he'd say, always pouring himself one too.

One day I was the last in a string of several students. Sensei, with cheeks already glowing red, ceremoniously poured our drinks. Both sitting in seiza, we toasted and drank.

The first twenty minutes of my lesson went more or less as it always did. He listened and corrected my homework, then asked me to play "Rokudan" by myself from beginning to end. I had by now memorized the first two sections of the piece and was eager and excited to show him I could play it alone.

Fueled with sake confidence, I began the piece. My tempo was a little slow, but I thought I was playing brilliantly. Yamada stared blankly at me as I moved through my memorized sections into the next four parts. With a few minutes left in the piece, I raised my eyes, hoping to see a glow of approval on Sensei's face. Instead I saw a sleeping figure nodding and wavering, battling against unconsciousness. A grin came over my face, immediately turning the next note into a high-pitched whistle. Wondering what to do, I decided to increase my volume as much as possible to bring him back. Unfortunately I'd lost him. Suddenly his body started slumping forward, and bit by bit, he folded in half and ended up in a very awkward position with his face flat on the floor. He was fast asleep, and, with the accompaniment of his snorts and grunts, I played on.

After nine months of intense daily practice, I reached a point where Yamada said he had gone as far as he could with me. He knew I wanted to study the more complicated Zen honkyoku music, and he recommended a player named Sasaki. Apparently Sasaki was a "man of Zen" and an extremely strict teacher who practiced suizen, or "blowing Zen."

At my last lesson Yamada explained that he had taught me to use the full twelve notes of the chromatic range and that, with Sasaki, I would learn the many microtones between each note. Honkyoku pieces, he explained, needed the precision of techniques that make this instrument different from all others. To learn them, he said, required a great deal of practice and control, and a good sense of pitch.

He had made all the necessary arrangements for my first lesson with Sasaki Sensei and handed me a detailed map of how to get to his studio. Looking a little sad, he asked me to keep him informed periodically of my progress, if I had time.

My leaving was a landmark occasion for Yamada, as I was his first student to be recommended to study with a master. He said the "chair leg" would have to go, then brought out one of his older bamboo shakuhachi and gave it to me as a gift.

"In return I want you to become a fine player, Ray-san, a player with heart."

I was speechless.

Sasaki, my new teacher, lived west of Tokyo in a city called Hachioji. On my first visit, I arrived at the station thirty minutes early, with the knowledge that no matter how precise Yamada's map was, the studio would still be hard to find. And it was!

Flustered and sweating, I arrived five minutes late. There was a handwritten note taped to the door that read:

Mr. Ray Blooks, come into my room please.

I opened the door and saw Sasaki sitting on a cushion in seiza with his eyes closed. I noticed a blue cushion placed about ten feet from him. I quickly kicked off my shoes and made an energetic dash for it. Not considering the highly polished floor, I went sliding in my socked feet and crashed to the ground. As I went down, I clipped the cushion and sent it whizzing towards Sasaki. *Shit!* Clutching my knapsack to my chest, I staggered to my feet, too embarrassed to rub my throbbing elbow.

As calmly as possible, I said, "Good morning, Sensei."

He returned my greeting and asked if I was okay.

"Fine," I said, as I retrieved the cushion from under his nose and placed it in its original position.

"Please, sit down."

The room became quiet, and the only sound that could be heard now was the fast pace of my breathing. Sasaki waited until I regained my composure, then he introduced himself. Barely giving me time to respond, he abruptly began to outline his philosophy and his method of teaching. As he spoke I could see there was an unmistakable air of condescension about him. I wondered if we'd be able to get along.

He wore the traditional *samue* outfit of black, baggy pants with a short kimono-style jacket. His hair was long and straggly, and his head was balding.

From his words and actions, there wasn't any doubt that he was a purist. He had an acute dislike of anyone who used lacquer in the barrel of their flutes and told me he was dedicated to the pure sound of Zen shakuhachi. He believed the bamboo should be dug out of the ground, cured, drilled, filed, then played. The other school of thought preferred lacquer in the barrel, saying that it gave a vividness to the tone color and volume. The flute that Yamada had given me had the dreaded lacquer in it, but because I was a beginner, Sasaki made an exception for me. Still, I was always reminded that players who used lacquer flutes didn't follow the "true way."

By the end of the first lesson that day, I realized that Sasaki was a passionate teacher and a formidable character. Perhaps as a warning, he told me that if his students weren't hardworking and totally serious about the "art of shakuhachi," they should find another teacher.

Each of Sasaki's lessons started with fifteen minutes of zazen meditation. At the end of the zazen, we would change our position and kneel in seiza. Thankfully, both positions were now a little easier for me. After zazen he would, without fail, tell me that shakuhachi was "too much difficult," and then we'd begin blowing long tones for fifteen minutes. The remainder of each lesson was spent studying a honkyoku piece. For the first two months we worked mainly on a classical composition called "Honshirabe," which means "Original Piece."

"This piece can make friendship between bamboo and player," Sasaki told me, "but must study too much."

Sasaki liked to speak English during the lesson. Nearly all of his sentences started with either "good" or "bad."

"Good shakuhachi player play with head move side and side. Bad shakuhachi player play with head move down to up" was one of his regular sayings. Another favorite was "Bad shakuhachi player play the honkyoku with bad pitch and call it Zen." And there was always, "Good shakuhachi player don't use the lacquer shakuhachi." Thankfully both his and my respective language abilities improved over time.

Sasaki frequently reminded me that shakuhachi grew directly out of the ground and started life as a straw. Students, he said, should appreciate this and understand the process by which a piece of bamboo is dug up with its roots intact and transformed into a flute. All of his flutes, he said, were related, coming from the same *madake* bamboo grove. Each grove was one single organism, and the roots of every tree connected beneath the ground in an intricate system of capillaries.

As part of his mandatory curriculum, his students were expected to participate in at least one bamboo-gathering expedition. This event took place a couple of times during the autumn months each year.

One rainy Saturday in mid-October, equipped with shovels and saws, five fellow students, Sasaki, and I squelched through the mud heading towards a bamboo grove to hunt for the perfect flute. We had already been instructed in what to look for. Thickness, node spacing, color, and marking characteristics were the criteria in selecting what would become the finished product.

We covered an area of about one square mile, finding and digging up ten suitable pieces.

The next morning we were back in Sasaki's workshop, watching him carefully heat each piece over a low flame, releasing the natural oils and turning the bamboo from green to a golden brown. These pieces, he told us, would be dried in the sunlight for up to two weeks, then aged for three years. In the afternoon we were each given a cured piece of bamboo to make a shakuhachi. Three students reclaimed bamboo, which they had dug up from a previous year's outing. We measured, cut, drilled, shaped, and filed the bamboo under the watchful eye of Sasaki. There was a student concert that evening and, no matter how rudimentary your flute, you were expected to perform on it in front of invited guests. A daunting task. These flutes didn't have anywhere near the precision and balance of the professionally made lacquer-filled shakuhachi. That night I blew a dissonant, muffled, and sometimes silent rendition of "Honshirabe."

Sasaki's background was a mystery to me. All I knew about him was that he was a shakuhachi master who had started his own Zen sect. I once asked him about his lineage but his answer was vague, only implying that he was influenced by an old shakuhachi and Zen master called Watazumi, but hadn't met him. He never once mentioned whom he had studied with. Curious to find out, I asked a couple of his students if they knew anything. They weren't sure, saying that he had never talked about other teachers. One did say that he thought he had studied with a famous master many years ago but had left to start his own sect.

Sasaki recommended that while studying music, I should also learn about the history of shakuhachi and its links to Zen. He said familiarizing myself with other Zen arts and studying the works of some of the great Zen masters and poets would give me a better understanding of my own art. *My own art.* I liked the sound of that.

Sasaki idolized some of the Zen masters, whom he liked to call Zen rebels. He said that I should study them and suggested that I read the works of Bassui, Ikkyu, Bankei, Basho, and Ryokan. He explained that all were great Zen teachers, poets, and calligraphers. They were men who had either deeply challenged or completely rejected the ideology of their day. Unable to find truth within the dogma of the great monasteries, they decided to look within themselves, many becoming hermits or wandering pilgrims in their search for an authentic life. I wasn't sure how much of this information would help my playing, but the notion of Zen rebels intrigued me.

The fifteenth-century Zen rebel Ikkyu especially caught my attention. Not just because of his unconventional lifestyle, or the fact that he played and wrote poems about the shakuhachi, but because his poetry was defiant, uncompromising, and inflammatory. Most of the verse expressed sorrow at the corruption of Zen or lashed out at the hierarchical order of the day. Many poems were about his fascination with sexual love. His claim that truth is to be found in everyday actions and not in religious orthodoxy made a lot of sense to me.

At the age of twenty-six, while drifting in a boat and meditating, Ikkyu experienced enlightenment on hearing the sudden caw of a crow. After that, he chose to live as a hermit and was often seen wandering aimlessly around the countryside near Kyoto, wearing ragged robes and straw sandals, his hair and beard growing wild. He played shakuhachi by the roadside well into his seventies.

In 1474, no longer able to avoid the appointment, he was ordained as the Abbot of Daitoku-ji, one of the great monasteries of Kyoto. Even then he elected to live in a small temple in his own village of Maki.

Sasaki told me that Ikkyu continues to be somewhat of a folk hero in Japan, something I can't quite understand. If alive today, he would surely have been completely ostracized for his uncompromising views on materialism and his relentless attacks on the decadence and widespread corruption in politics and business.

Sasaki often used the lives of the Zen rebels to illustrate a point when answering my questions. Once I foolishly asked about the grading and certification system in the different shakuhachi sects. As usual, I waited while he furiously searched through his dictionary for key words. Once he found them, he'd write them down on the pad beside him, then, unwittingly piece them together and come up with something rather interesting.

"Certification is the mandate of fools," he bellowed out. "Is it possible to have passion without a cause, to play shakuhachi, or do anything for that matter, for its own sake and not merely for status?"

Visibly ruffled, he then went on to tell me the tale of how the rebellious Ikkyu tore up his certificate of confirmation as a Zen master in utter disapproval at the corruption of Zen. Ikkyu also refused to confirm or certify enlightenment in any of his students.

Sasaki agreed with his actions wholeheartedly and went on to explain how most people attached such importance to the end result, their concern being only with measured success and not with the beauty of simply learning.

There were times, I must admit, when he went over the top about his Japanese wandering rebels and their uniqueness. On these occasions I felt compelled to counterattack, tossing in my own personal favorite rebels—everyone I could think of from Socrates to Jack Kerouac. A typical infuriating rebuttal from Sasaki would be "Ah yes, but if only Camus and Nietzsche had been able to meet a Zen master, they could have turned that existentialism into a way to live."

I once threw in Blake, who was one of England's own brilliant prophets. I told Sasaki about his first literary work, *Songs of Innocence,* and his marvelous painting *Ancient of Days.* This painting, I explained, is, to me, so full of intelligence and power, suggesting that one should face reality. This British visionary and dreamer wandered all over London, and, on one occasion, found himself in a hamlet south of the city. It was here that he looked up into a tree and saw a vision of angels. When I told Sasaki about this, he raised an eyebrow and began frantically flipping through his dictionary.

"Angels, angels . . . trick . . . trick. Sounds like Blake-san suffered from . . . delusion," said Sasaki.

I laughed and thought of my favorite line from one of Blake's poems:

May God us keep from single vision and Newton's sleep.

杉
風
之
調

Chapter Eight
Water Seekers
and Worshippers

The inescapable stress and strain of life in Tokyo were draining me. Dianne was fairing better; although often exhausted from all the commuting, she was at least enjoying her work. I loathed mine. English teaching for me was just a means to an end. Dianne's work was varied. She was teaching, but she had also landed quite a bit of voice work, thanks to her distinct British accent. She was recording audiotapes for English language textbooks and other events. One contract she was working on was an English voice-over recording for a well-known theater group. It was for a Japanese theatrical performance that was going to the Royal Edinburgh Festival. Dianne's English language students were mostly quite interesting people. She taught some company presidents, a few television celebrities, an up and coming soccer star, and some highly motivated women who wanted to become bilingual flight attendants. Whereas my lot were mostly mentally exhausted university and college students or salarimen who didn't want to be there but had to attend.

Between this work and visiting Sasaki for my shakuhachi lessons, I managed to continue practicing regularly at Arai Yakushi Temple.

It had been the end of the monsoon and the beginning of the hot season when I first started playing there. By this point, I'd witnessed all the season's offerings several times—from spring blossoms and typhoons to bitter frost and snow.

Every practice session began with a short calming ritual. I started by sitting on the verandah with my eyes closed, counting deep breaths from one to ten. Each count had a complete cycle of inhalation and exhalation. On cold days, I circled the temple building performing this same breathing exercise until I was warm.

This type of breathing usually stilled the noise in my head and put me in the right frame of mind for practicing. Sasaki always said that without deep, intelligent breath, there would be no suizen or meditation.

When I'd completed my breathing exercises, I spent the next forty-five minutes blowing long tones on each note.

In the beginning, the locals and visitors kept their distance from me, either out of shyness or, more likely, out of a deep-rooted fear and distrust of all foreigners—feelings that likely go back to their first encounters with those "butter-smelling" barbarians from the outside world. Sometimes when I played, my eyes would meet with the eyes of a passerby who, caught in the act of looking at me, would be forced, out of politeness to pause and give a slight, acknowledging bow.

I was always approached with the most extraordinary civility—a degree of courtesy and politeness that I hadn't experienced in any other country. This Japanese manner, bordering on obsequiousness and submission, is the result of hundreds of years of obedience to the once-ruling samurai warrior class. Samurai were overzealous rulers who had developed a highly refined and ritualized code of etiquette. They were obsessed with perfection at all levels and demanded it from their subjects. One breach of this complicated code or any change in facial expression, and the poor violator was taken care of with a samurai sword. Their power was unlimited and greatly feared by all. The samurai's code of etiquette gradually seeped down to their subordinates, and still exists in a diluted form to this day.

Over time, I became less of a spectacle to the temple visitors, and more of a fixture. A few of the regulars would call out "Gambatte kudasai," in the same way that the head monk did every day. Some passersby initiated small conversations. They probed politely with questions about my shakuhachi studies, trying to establish if I was a serious student or if what I was doing was just a mere pastime. I knew that the Japanese had little respect for dabblers and admired anyone who "diligently" stuck with their chosen goal, hence the encouraging cry "Gambatte!"

The flute broke down the usual problems of language and cultural barriers, and because of it, I was able to meet people from all walks of life. People who would normally avoid foreigners were soon nourishing me with gifts of fruit, and warming me with hot sake and lively conversation.

Arai Yakushi Temple was well known in the area for its underground source of spring water, which the locals believed had great healing qualities. One of the people who came regularly to fill plastic bottles was a lovely old woman, who later became known to me as Hanna-san. Hanna-san first approached me because I was practicing a seasonal piece during the wrong season. It was too much for her to bear hearing me play "Haru no Umi," which means "Spring Sea," in the depths of winter. Exasperated, she came over to correct my error.

"*Dam-e! Dam-e!* Not good! Not good!" she said, waving her hand from side to side. "This is a Japanese song we play only in springtime."

I apologized for my ignorance, and this seemed to satisfy her. I continued to practice many seasonal pieces out of season, but was always careful to change when I saw her coming.

Hanna-san was eighty-five years old, and sadly, had an awful stoop, which was most likely the result of hard work and poor nutrition during the war years. With the aid of an old hand-carved walking stick, she was able to support herself and maintain a reasonably stable forty-five degree angle. Her skin was weathered and dusted with freckles and age spots. When she lifted her head to talk, I could see deep furrows running down from the corners of her mouth. These gave her the appearance of a carved puppet. She always wore a traditional plain gray or brown kimono, and her silver hair was pulled back in a tidy but unfashionable bun.

As a gaijin I was regarded as something of a novelty by Hanna-san. She always treated me graciously in a kind of bossy, grandmotherly way. During that winter, she often told me that I didn't have enough clothing on and that I was too thin. When the weather turned warm again, she'd bring me water from the nearby well, telling me that I must drink at least six cups a day.

Some days, when Hanna-san was in the mood to chat, she stayed longer than usual. I enjoyed these visits. I would put down my flute, get comfortable on the old wooden steps, and listen, trying to follow her Japanese and pick out as many words as I could. She liked to tell me about the old days and, invariably, her conversation always came around to the decline of modern Japanese youth. She disliked the way this new breed of Japanese were acting, and said they had forsaken all of the old values in the pursuit of material wealth. From what I could gather, she thought that young men today put personal and outside interests before family and work. Women, she said, had completely lost their way and were no longer interested in dedicating themselves to their families.

"They don't remember the war," she said, "the great hardship and sacrifice we all experienced. Young people no longer work for the good of all. They only live for themselves these days. Japan only has these," she said, holding out her crippled old hands, blue veins showing through the transparent skin. "We have nothing else—the wealth could be gone tomorrow!" she grumbled.

Hanna-san was right. Many of the old ways were disappearing. In the early 1980s, the youth were hugely impressed and excited by the American lifestyle and were desperately trying to emulate it through their outward attitude and dress. Their role models became Tom Cruise, Sylvester Stallone, Madonna, and other popular icons of the day. But beneath the baseball caps, Ray-bans, Levi's and designer accessories lay a thousand years of cultural conditioning.

From talking to some of these young people, I'd discovered that they didn't have anywhere near the same passion or loyalty for work that their parents had. They told me that what they wanted was freedom from duty, along with a private life full of leisure and pleasure. Work was only a means to an end. They wanted to be individuals. In their efforts to achieve this individuality, they merely created a new kind of groupism with an unconvincing fabricated appearance about it. No matter how they acted or what they wore, that unmistakable essence of Japaneseness always managed to make itself evident through their mannerisms. There were occasions while I was talking to Hanna-san at the temple when a group of these "new-style" Japanese youth would pass us. I can't remember one instance when they didn't bow upon eye contact, even if it was just a slight unconscious nod.

Aside from the water collectors at the temple, many regular visitors were, of course, worshippers. Each evening, among them, were always a few young men and women who visited the temple on their way home from work. They often said a prayer in front of a life-size statue of a Bodhisattva. A Bodhisattva renounces entry into Buddhahood until all sentient beings are saved. Dressed in "up-to-the-minute-fashions," they carefully poured water on the Bodhisattva and scrubbed furiously at points on its body that corresponded to ailments in their own bodies. This was believed to cure or alleviate the complaints. The stone figure was worn away, especially on his head, stomach, and lower back.

Worshippers also visited an enormous cast iron incense burner in front of the steps to the main temple building. They lit bunches of incense and placed them in the old ash. The burner was always bellowing with smoke, giving the temple a wonderful musky smell that frequently reminded me that I was in Asia. With the same purpose as scrubbing the statue, people wafted the incense smoke onto their ailing body parts. Hanna-san always insisted that I scrub the Bodhisattva's chest and waft incense smoke onto my hands and throat.

One afternoon while I practiced at the temple, a huge, black, fully loaded four-wheel drive entered the temple grounds. The driver, a very trendy-looking man dressed in cowboy boots, designer jeans, a baseball cap, and leather jacket, jumped out. His passenger, a Shinto priest dressed in a long white robe, tall black hat, and huge wooden clogs, got out of the other side. The young man removed his sunglasses, and, walking like James Dean, went to the front of the temple.

He coolly threw a few coins into the donation box, bowed his head, clapped his hands twice, and said a fairly quick prayer. Then he turned and walked down the steps to the large cast-iron burner, and started fanning smoke from the already burning incense in the direction of his eyes, even bending slightly to make sure the smoke made contact. And it did. Pulling a handkerchief from his pocket, tears miraculously started streaming down his face. The Arai Yakushi Temple is famous for its benevolent Buddha of Eyesight.

While the young man was at the incense burner, the Shinto priest clopped around the vehicle in a counterclockwise direction, muttering a prayer and waving what seemed to be a wand with strips of white cloth attached to the end. Each side of the truck was getting a jolly good blessing. Within twenty minutes, the priest finished performing his duties, the cool guy's eyes stopped streaming, and they both drove off in the newly consecrated vehicle.

The meaning of these daily rituals was explained to me by a retired university professor, who dismissed it all as superstition. However, he regularly came to the temple to light a candle and pray. And on the odd occasion, I noticed—if no one was around and I seemed absorbed in my playing—he would scrub the Bodhisattva on his stomach and then walk over to the incense burner and waft smoke on his head.

One day, the professor appeared just as Hanna-san was presenting me with a small bag of Japanese oranges. As usual, she was chastising me, this time for not eating enough fruit, and for wearing a short-sleeved shirt out of season. I often wondered if there was a special day in Japan when one changed from long-sleeved to short. There probably was, and, no doubt, the occasion would have a name. Scolding me was something Hanna-san enjoyed, and I took it as her way of showing affection.

Coming towards us, the professor seeing the scene enthusiastically called out, "Komuso! Komuso!"

Hanna-san, delighted by what he'd said, laughed and said, "Gaijin komuso!" which loosely translates to "*foreign* wandering monk of nothingness and emptiness." They both thought this was hilarious and laughed together at the peculiar image they had conjured up.

Hanna-san must have mentioned the "gaijin komuso" joke while shopping in the local marketplace. From that day on, the *tofu* maker, the bread baker, the fruit and veggie vendors, and many others referred to me as the "gaijin komuso."

Chapter Nine
Temple Sensei

Feeling lightheaded but incredibly satisfied after a long afternoon of practice, I sat quietly on the temple verandah. The rain was finally easing off, and the clouds were starting to clear in the west.

The temple cats appeared at their regular time, their coats patchy and grimy. I watched them for a few minutes and then noticed a tall portly man in a dark gray suit approaching the verandah. There was an air of position and authority in his walk, and he looked as if he were very high up in the corporate world.

He came to a halt about ten feet away.

"Hello. How are you? Please come closer," I offered. He'd caught me at a good time.

"You . . . good sound, good . . . pitch," he said, as he walked up to me.

"Do you play shakuhachi?" I asked.

He nodded modestly but looked unsure.

"I hear shakuhachi in market," he said, smiling and cupping his ear with his hand.

I hadn't realized the flute could be heard from such a distance and over such noisy traffic. He shyly glanced at the music I had wedged into the frame of the temple window. With a quizzical look, he craned his neck forward to read the title.

"That one," I said, pointing to the temple window, "is called 'Sanya.' It describes musically a monk's search for enlightenment." I hesitated, realizing my English wasn't being completely understood. I took the sheet of music down from the window and pointed at the notation.

"See, here are the climaxes. That's why it's called 'Sanya,' or 'Three Valleys,'" I said.

He looked impressed. Feeling I was on a roll, I picked up my folder containing all the other pieces I was studying.

"This is called 'Shika no Tone.' It represents the sound of two deer calling to one another, and is usually played by two shakuhachi." I played the first few notes.

"Sugoi," he cried. There was a look of amazement on his face.

None of my usual visitors or onlookers had ever shown this kind of interest. His enthusiasm prompted me to search through my folder and find a piece of music that I thought might really impress him.

"This is 'Tsuro no Sugomori.' It's the most difficult piece. Many of the special trills and flutters imitate the sound of a bird. Listen." I picked up the flute and proceeded to warble with my throat, then, imitating the movements of a crane, puffed out my chest and flapped my arms.

More "sugoi's" were uttered.

"And this one is called 'Tamuke.' It's a kind of offering or prayer to Buddha."

"Your teacher is who?" he asked, halting me in midflow.

"Sasaki Sensei in Hachioji," I replied.

"Sasaki, Sasaki! I am . . . teacher . . . old student him," he said.

"Really? You studied with Sasaki Sensei in Hachioji?" I asked excitedly.

He looked confused. The conversation was becoming too much for him, so he removed his wallet, pulled out a name card, and offered it to me. I took it in the customary and respectful way, with both hands. I glanced at the card and saw that it was written in kanji and placed it on top of my music folder, then apologized for not having a card to give him. We thanked each other and said good-bye.

Hearing the 5:00 electronic chimes sound out across Nakano, I decided it was time to gather up my stuff and leave. As I took out my wallet to put away my visitor's card, I noticed that English was written on the back of it. It said:

KATSUYA YOKOYAMA
President of the Shakuhachi Society

I was dumbfounded.

"Oh my God!" I laughed out loud. "I just gave Katsuya Yokoyama an introductory lesson!"

What an idiot! I thought as I stumbled to get my things together. Yokoyama hadn't studied with Sasaki; it had been the other way around. Yokoyama was Sasaki's mysterious teacher. Sasaki, wanting to start his own sect, had obviously stopped

97

studying with Yokoyama before he had been certified, hence the hostility against certification. Shaking my head in amazement at it all, I quickly put away my music—music that Yokoyama had recorded and played a thousand times. I experienced alternating waves of elation and acute embarrassment.

Running home, all I could think about was telling Dianne about my meeting and getting my Japanese friend Yumiko to call Yokoyama and apologize for something. I wasn't quite sure what exactly. First I telephoned Dianne at work. The receptionist said that she was in class. I thanked her, hung up, and immediately called Yumiko and explained what had just happened. She was astonished at the coincidence, but persuading her to make the phone call wasn't easy. She worried that Yokoyama might be offended by her lack of protocol. After a little gentle urging, she said she'd call. As soon as I hung up, the telephone rang. It was Dianne.

"What's up? They came to get me out of class. They said you sounded anxious."

"Oh. Sorry. But something really amazing just happened, and I wanted to tell you straight away."

She could hardly believe my story and said I should definitely follow up and make contact with him again. With that I told her that Yumiko was calling him right now on my behalf.

Yumiko was excited when she called back thirty minutes later.

"Ray-san, Yokoyama was very happy to see you at the temple. At first he thought that it was the public address system he could hear. You are very lucky to meet such a man. And, Ray-san, he has invited you to go to his studio for a lesson when you feel you are ready to. You must not miss such an opportunity."

"He said I could have a lesson!" I replied.

"Yes. Maybe I think this means you can be his student. And, Ray-san, I introduced myself to him as your 'interpreter,' and he suggested that I go with you to help with translation," she said excitedly.

"Would you, Yumiko?" I asked.

"Yes, of course, and guess what? His studio is only five minutes from your home, Ray-san!"

"I know," I said. "I saw the address on his card. I can hardly believe it." I'd been traveling one and a half hours each way on the train to see Sasaki, while only five minutes away from my house and practice place was one of the greatest shakuhachi players and teachers in the world.

I felt that the opportunity to study with Yokoyama could be a real turning point for me, but once again thoughts of leaving Japan came strongly to mind. I wanted more than anything to study with him, but I knew that both Dianne and I were beginning to show definite signs of fatigue.

That evening we talked about what we thought we should do. If we stayed longer, would we know when it was time to leave, or would we end up like some of the foreigners we'd met who had stayed too long? I ran into many burnt-out teachers who were filled with cynicism and bitterness, not just towards their students but towards all that was Japanese, but none of them wanted to give up the large sums of money they were earning. They were always two or three months away from their leaving date.

Dianne was truly excited about the prospect of my studying with Yokoyama and, once again, said that if I was still enjoying it as much as ever, then there was no choice but to carry on. I was enjoying it, there was no doubt about that, but the teaching and standard of living were getting me down. With this in mind, Dianne suggested that we take a long overdue break for a few months and go to India.

"We'll rent a little cottage in the foothills of the Himalayas for a while," she said, adding that she'd reorganize her schedule and would ask a couple of her girlfriends to take some of her students while she was away. I'd just quit my job and get another one when we returned.

"We'll recharge our batteries, Ray, and get a fresh perspective on what we're both doing here. When we come back we'll both lighten up our schedules a bit and slow down," she said enthusiastically. "You can practice shakuhachi as much as you like in India and breathe the freshest air possible at the same time." Then, congratulating herself, she said, "Who would have thought that that little piece of plumber's pipe would lead to an invitation to study with the number one player in Japan!"

So it was decided. We'd sublet our room to a friend and head for the Himalayas. But before we could, I had another dilemma to solve: How could I move on without offending Sasaki? I telephoned my old teacher, Yamada, and relayed the story of my serendipitous meeting. He was thrilled and said that, over the years, he'd seen Yokoyama Sensei many times in concert but had never had the chance to meet him. He said I shouldn't ignore this meeting, but should simply explain it all to Sasaki. I felt the pressure of Japanese etiquette biting at my heels, but knew I had to take this opportunity. We didn't have another five years of Japan in us.

When I entered Sasaki's studio the next day, I had absolutely no idea what I would say. I'd thought so much about it my mind was a blank. Sasaki was an excellent teacher, and in a culture where people were expected to "do their time" and "pay their dues," he had allowed me, over the last eighteen months, to progress rapidly, never holding anything back. His instruction had gone way beyond the confines of an ordinary shakuhachi lesson. I felt guilty about leaving him. Unfaithful even.

After the lesson finished, owing him the complete truth, I simply told him the whole story of how I'd met Yokoyama in the temple, omitting the fact that I now knew who his teacher had been. I could see no point in embarrassing him. Anyway, I didn't know all the facts, but I guessed that he didn't want to live in the shadow of Yokoyama.

"Ray-san," he said, immediately rescuing me. "Yokoyama, very good lacquer shakuhachi player. You like the lacquer. You want to stay with the lacquer, I know. You change to Yokoyama lacquer."

He went on to tell me I had progressed well under his tuition and that he expected great things from me.

杉
風
之
調

Chapter Ten
Grand Master

Rested and refreshed from our trip to India, I was excited about meeting with Yokoyama and having my first lesson with him. The three-month break had done us both good, and we felt ready to resume our work and studies again.

It was 5:30 in the afternoon when I left the temple and walked through the bustling market crowd towards my apartment. I needed to take a shower and change my clothes before meeting Yumiko and heading to Yokoyama's studio.

The Market Street was called Arai Yakushi Ginza after the temple. This little shopping area was a great example of how the Tokyo residents have managed to keep the intimate village atmosphere alive. Tokyo is made up of hundreds of village communities, each one virtually identical to the other. You could find these traditional markets in every single residential area throughout the city, and country, for that matter.

Arai Yakushi Ginza was a narrow street, seasonally decorated with overhead lights and pink plastic cherry blossoms in the spring, and with colorful flowers in the summer. Orange, red, and brown sprigs of leaves in the fall, followed by gold, silver, and green arrangements in the winter. The four seasons of nature's splendor were well represented. On special holidays, the street's public address system would broadcast traditional festival music.

The shops, some little more than market stalls, were colorful and inviting. The tofu shop was always my first stop of the day. I'd pick up a cup of warm, freshly made soymilk there. The maker and his wife found it quite amusing that I liked it so much, and they told me almost every time how few Japanese cared for the natural type anymore, preferring instead the flavored types at the supermarket. The *miso* shop opposite was very old-fashioned, and displayed all the different types of miso, a fermented soybean paste, in large wooden vats.

There was a small electrical shop, with its little satellite dishes and tiny, apartment-sized appliances. The bakery, in addition to selling fresh-baked bread and cakes, made potato salad sandwiches and meat donuts. After several visits to the market, the couple at the fruit and vegetable stand got to know Dianne and me and always gave us extra little treats when we bought something. "Service," they'd say, smiling.

Feeling reinvigorated from my shower, I left the apartment and walked back through the market towards the station. On my way down the arcade, I noticed a very distinguished-looking man carrying a long, tubelike container. I wondered if he was also headed to Yokoyama's studio. A pang of nervousness cascaded through me.

I had spent the entire day practicing at the temple in anticipation of that evening's lesson, but as the time grew closer, familiar waves of doubt swept through me. I wondered if I was ready to learn from Yokoyama. But most of all, I was nervous about the prospect of playing in front of other shakuhachi students. I'd heard that some of Yokoyama's students had been studying with him for more than twenty years and that many of them performed regularly around the city. During the day, I had conjured up mental images of myself sitting in his studio, frozen with fear, breath and lip control completely gone, Yokoyama and his students patiently waiting.

I arrived at the station early, fifteen minutes before I was supposed to meet Yumiko. Among the teeming mass of commuters, I knew she would easily spot me. There were only two foreigners there, myself and a street musician named "Two-Note Tony," who was doing his usual impersonation of a harmonica player. Tony had been named "Two-Note" by the local foreigners because that's all he played: two notes, suck and blow. He never attempted to move up or down the scale, just the same two notes over and over again.

Over time, Tony and I had become familiar with each other, with a few casual words in passing eventually growing into conversations.

Tony was a huge, odorous man with a round, red unshaven face. He wore the same filthy clothes every day. His old suit trousers were covered in stains and three inches too short, exposing his soiled, bare ankles. The buttons of his once-white shirt had busted away, liberating his massive white belly. It was hard to tell, but I guessed he was in his late forties or early fifties.

When he wasn't performing, his mouth hung open, revealing a mouthful of teeth that were beyond repair. His mousy gray hair was oily, unbrushed, and clumped into mats.

The sight of Two-Note Tony may not have caused much of a stir in the West, but here, surrounded by the freshly washed, scrubbed, and immaculate Japanese, he was a definite abnormality.

People tried not to look at Tony, but for most, the temptation was too great. To the Japanese he was too fascinating to miss, so they cautiously and discreetly stole glimpses of him with disbelieving eyes. Tony was impervious to their silent gasps and no longer saw people. He simply stared straight ahead with vacant eyes, likely dreaming of the hamburger special he would buy once he'd raised enough cash. I knew he loved his burgers because I saw him almost daily, sitting in the McDonald's in the nearby shopping arcade. The restaurant was usually full, but there was always available seating within Tony's odor zone. Customers avoided him like he had something you could catch.

As usual, Tony had positioned himself near the station's ticket machines—a good tactic. People in the ticket lineups were always handling their change. Sometimes some of it found its way into Tony's grubby hat, which was placed on the ground in front of him. Beside his hat were three filthy teddy bears, which were no doubt a part of his act.

I approached Tony and watched him for a while. He puffed out his signature two-note piece for about two minutes, then he stopped, bowed west, then north, then east. With each bow, he said, "Domo arigato. Thank you." Then he banged the harmonica on his trouser leg, adding to an unsightly damp patch that indicated he'd been there for quite a while.

I placed some loose change in his hat and noticed that the three little bears were in need of some serious medical attention. One had no arms, another had only one eye and one ear, and the third had a huge gash on its leg with stuffing hanging out. Mixed in with his earnings was a train ticket and a stick of gum.

"Hello, Ray. How're you doing?" he asked, his eyes adjusting their focal length to meet my face.

As we spoke, a couple of young girls walked by, both wearing navy blue and white sailor-style school uniforms. They stopped, looked down at the abused teddies, and in high-pitched, cartoonlike voices cried, "*Kawai so! Kawai so!* Poor things!"

Tony turned his attention towards them and made a playful growling sound. The girls grabbed onto each other and scampered away.

"There's a train ticket in your hat, Tony. Someone's dropping you a hint," I said in jest.

"Bollocks! Bollocks to them all!" he replied vehemently.

I asked how he was.

"Not so bad. You can't complain. Well, actually you can, but no bastard will listen to you," he said flatly, then started ranting on about how the station employees were trying to move him on. "Bastards," he muttered. He'd been at this location for four months, and before that he'd been ousted from Ikebukuro Station. He relayed this story to me for the third time and ended it with "Bloody fascists. Sod 'em."

I never quite worked out how Tony managed to survive in the most expensive city in the world. He once told me that he had first come to Japan ten years ago from Sheffield, England, to teach English. He'd photocopied a friend's arts degree in philosophy, whited-out the name, and typed in his own. He said that in those days, that's all you needed.

It was true. Backpackers would arrive from various parts of Asia and buy a photocopied degree within hours of landing, then work until they'd raised enough travel money to head out again. Some had kept this up for years. I met a barely understandable cockney lad from the East End of London who had a degree from the University of California. I asked him where he'd brought it from. "I got it from a mate, didn't I," he told me, tapping his nose.

Tony said he came to find a Japanese wife. He told me he had read somewhere that Japanese women made excellent wives. "I left my taxi driving job and all me pub mates, and off I went in search of Madam Butterfly, never once thinking to check the local Japanese restaurant before I left," Tony explained

"Revolutionary idea for a Sheffield boy in those days, Ray," he said. "Within three years I had the wife and the job, but it was all downhill from there. For the first while, she served me hand and foot, didn't she. Even put toothpaste on me brush in the mornings. By heck, those were grand days," he reminisced. "It was two weeks after the honeymoon that I noticed the horns growing out the side of her head."

Tony lost his teaching job two months after the wedding. Apparently he'd struck one of the Japanese staff and was instantly dismissed. Soon his wife also dismissed him. She now lived in England, working in one of London's Japanese restaurants.

"How's the shakuhachi coming along, Ray?"

"Slowly, Tony, very slowly. I'm just off for a lesson actually. I'm starting with a new teacher tonight."

When he had first asked me what I was doing in Japan, I said that apart from teaching English, I was studying the shakuhachi. "Ah! Shakuhachi, the sound of wisdom," he had remarked. "Do you play folk songs or classical shakuhachi?"

I told him I was studying the original style, which was called honkyoku.

"That's a good choice, mate. I like the Zen pieces best."

On the surface, Two-Note looked like the local village idiot, but I had discovered on several occasions that not only was he incredibly insightful and well-read, but also had really interesting stories to tell.

Not long after we first met, he cajoled me into a discussion on existentialism right there in front of the ticket machines. Oblivious to his surroundings, he proceeded in the manner of a reincarnated Jean-Paul Sartre, but with spit flying and arms flailing. His loud attacks on the state of the human condition were merciless. I didn't fully participate in the discussion because I was conscious of the scene we were creating. I just wanted it to end. My acquiescence to his every point didn't appease him. Any arguments I did make were met with a ruthless analysis of the human situation and a quick quotation by Nietzsche or Heidegger.

It was hard to believe that this unkempt harmonica player I now watched was the same man. Yumiko finally emerged from a sea of black hair and dark suits. She had just come from work and was dressed in a smart, conservative dark blue, winter suit and a blouse with a lace collar. Seeing Tony caught her off guard. A flicker of aversion in her face turned to a withdrawn and rather neutral expression.

"Ohisashiburi!" she quickly said. "Long time no see you, Ray-san. How are you?"

"I'm well, thank you. It's good to see you again. Yumiko, this is Two . . . eh . . . Tony."

With a bow, Tony greeted her in fluent Japanese. She didn't look too happy about meeting him, but nonetheless gave him a slight nod of a bow. Then I caught the look of horror on her face when her eyes settled on the three helpless, physically abused bears.

Yumiko suggested that we shouldn't be late. She obviously wanted to go, so we said good-bye to Tony and began the twenty-minute walk from the station to the studio. On the way there, we stopped off at a store and bought some *sembei,* or rice crackers, to take as a gift.

We arrived at the studio at 7:00 PM and entered after knocking. Eight pairs of shoes and one pair of cowboy boots were neatly parked just inside the door. I could hear voices but no music. I had visualized that Yokoyama's studio would be austere and simple, like Sasaki's place, with not much filling the room except for a scroll of calligraphy on the wall, a flower arrangement in an alcove, and priceless flutes displayed exquisitely on embroidered silk bags.

I was pleasantly relieved to find that Yokoyama's room was completely without affectation and was comfortably cluttered like a well-used home.

It must have been Yokoyama's break, as he was holding court. In sharp contrast to the first time I'd met him, he was now dressed more suitably for a country and western line dance than a shakuhachi lesson. He wore a red and black–checkered flannel shirt, and denim jeans with a large buckled belt. The boots at the door were obviously his.

Yokoyama and the students were all sitting crossed-legged around a long, low Japanese-style table that was overflowing with trays of sushi and other delicacies.

Yumiko and I introduced ourselves and exchanged the customary greetings. Yokoyama thanked me for the sembei and added it to the potluck feast. He seemed excited to see me again and explained to the students how we had first met and how this "temple sensei" had given him an introductory lesson. When he finished the story, everyone looked delighted and stared at me, nodding in amazement.

Then Yokoyama, smiling mischievously, asked his students to introduce themselves in English. Simultaneously each student made a sharp sucking noise through their teeth, which, roughly translated, means "very difficult." A palpable tension filled the room as they each waited their turn. For Japanese, speaking English in public is one of their biggest fears. I felt awful for them as they each struggled to tell me their name and occupation. The first to speak was the man I'd seen walking through the market. He said he was the president of a small company, and he apologized for not being able to study shakuhachi regularly because of all his work commitments. He then wished me luck with my studies.

One by one they suffered, each telling me a little about themselves. Two of the students explained that they were shakuhachi teachers with schools of their own.

As more students turned up that night, they were treated to the same tale of the "temple sensei" and his "introductory lesson." When Yokoyama spoke, he was incredibly animated, waving his arms to make a point. When he laughed this was the cue for everyone to laugh. I instantly liked him.

Once the spotlight was off me, I was able to settle myself and take in the surroundings. The studio was like so many Japanese rooms I'd been in. The place was filled with stuff that was piled high. In the teaching section of the studio, there was a rack displaying a dozen shakuhachi flutes, some of which were for sale and, on the floor, a large tool box. Within arm's reach of Yokoyama were his own flutes. In the student area at the back of the studio were boxes stacked up and filled with Yokoyama's instructional videotapes, compact discs, and audiotapes, all for sale.

On the floor were large envelopes filled with shakuhachi music, not the usual folded kind, but large stiff sheets. This music had been reproduced by Yokoyama and was for sale under his name. Seeing it, I had an awkward flashback to the "temple lesson" where the music I was using and showing him was his own, but photocopied!

I listened intently to all that was said, asking Yumiko to explain the parts I didn't understand. It was clear that the students thought of Yokoyama as more than just a teacher. They acted like they not only respected the man, but actually revered him. The role of sensei is not something taken lightly in Japan. With it comes immense social responsibility. For the Japanese the sensei is looked upon as a mentor, as someone to guide and direct you through life. It's not uncommon for a teacher to act as a counselor in a time of crisis, or even as a go-between when seeking a marriage partner. The student's part in the relationship is one of unconditional loyalty, diligence, and service.

After the sushi break, Yokoyama returned to his teaching position and summoned the next student. A man in his forties sitting next to me said, "Hai," immediately rose, excused himself from the group, and walked over to the student chair.

Seven students had already finished their lesson and were hanging around to listen. I was told I was next. I watched intently. The student approached Yokoyama deferentially, stooping slightly, flute in hand. I sensed that he was acutely aware of his peers behind him and this powerful person in front of him. He bowed deeply and sat down, adding an envelope to a pile of others. This was the traditional and polite way of paying fees.

The student unfolded his music and placed it on the table in front of himself. He waited a second or two, then exchanged another respectful bow with Yokoyama. Yumiko whispered to me all that she heard.

"Welcome, and thank you for coming."

"Thank you, Sensei."

One of the other students leaned over and asked Yumiko to tell me that this student was quite well known in the shakuhachi world. She quietly relayed the message, but I nodded to signal that I had understood.

Without hesitation, the student announced the piece he was about to play.

The same student near me leaned over again and said that this man had a concert coming up and this was one of the pieces on the program.

The student lifted the shakuhachi to his lips and paused before he began to play. The room was quiet. He drew a deep breath, then began. I could immediately hear Yokoyama's influence. The performance was hauntingly beautiful. Goose bumps rose on my arms.

Finishing the piece gracefully, the student returned the flute to his lap, bowed, then waited for comments. I was surprised when Yokoyama began asking the other students their opinions.

"Seki-san?"

"Very good, he made a great effort."

"Matama-san?"

"Very good effort. He must have worked hard."

"Furiya-san?"

"Excellent. He has put a great deal of work into his practice."

Yokoyama went all around the room, and then finally asked me my opinion.

"Ray-san?"

I was surprised that he asked me. I didn't think I was entitled to pass comment yet; I scrambled for something to say in Japanese but went blank.

"Er . . . fantastic . . . er . . . very proficient. Very well played," I answered.

"*Jouzu desu ne,*" said Yumiko, quickly summarizing my words into Japanese for me.

Yokoyama thanked us, then carefully, avoiding any form of direct criticism, gave his own constructive comments. These comments were achingly polite and indirect. He taught by the traditional method, which was with few words of instruction and with the student imitating the master's performance as closely as possible.

Yokoyama asked the student to play the piece again, but this time he would also play along with him. In this way, the student would be able to see his own weaknesses and strengths if he wished to. They started in unison, but I couldn't even hear the student. The power of Yokoyama was tremendous. Such grace, such beauty, a flurry of subtle finger movements. I savored the moment and felt fortunate to be there. After the piece ended and with a few more encouraging words from the master, the student bowed and returned to his place.

"Ray-san."

My stomach jumped. I rose to my feet and walked to the table. Yumiko followed. I bowed slightly and sat down. Yumiko knelt next to me on the floor. I placed my envelope on top of the others. Yokoyama bowed in gratitude, then we bowed to each other. But instead of asking me to play, he began talking about the music.

He said he was pleased that I had chosen to study honkyoku, adding that this style of music was very demanding and that the pieces were of a religious nature, to be respected. Each piece has been handed down from one individual to another for more than five hundred years.

"The depth of honkyoku music is found in a single tone, Ray-san."

I understood about twenty percent of what he said, so I was glad Yumiko had come. He paused while Yumiko translated, interrupting with his own English words that he felt confident with.

"Each phrase is played in one breath," he said. "Intensity of breath and control are most important. Sometimes we need an explosive blast of air, sometimes just a wisp. The beauty of the piece relies on the quality of your tone, color, perfect timing, and space." He then said it was important for each piece to be interpreted by the individual, becoming the player's own piece of music.

Yokoyama's curriculum was strictly followed. Once he was satisfied that you had memorized an assigned piece and could play it fairly well, you were given a new piece to study. In this way, the students were exposed to as many techniques as possible and would slowly build up their knowledge of Zen music. The music was learned in layers. Over the months and years students added layer upon layer to each piece as they became more adept. The pieces, therefore, became richer, more complex, and hopefully, as Yokoyama said, your own.

After correcting my posture and checking and advising me on a number of technical points, it was time to play. Yokoyama first asked me to blow *ro*. Ro is the lowest note, created when all five holes are closed. I blew with all the technique and power that I could muster. After I blew it three times each for twenty seconds, he stopped me. I was pleased with myself and expected some kind of congratulatory remark.

"Please play with more *ki*," Yokoyama said.

At this point Yumiko told Yokoyama that she wasn't sure how to explain ki in English. They conferred for a minute. Then Yumiko said that *ki* meant energy or spiritual strength.

This term was familiar to me. In China it is referred to as *chi* and in India as *prana*. In English perhaps we'd call it bioenergy. It's an ancient theory of the universal principle behind all life, the vital life force or absolute energy. The principle suggests that the oxygen we breathe is charged with ki, so that with optimum health, fitness, and awareness we can increase the intensity of this life-giving force in our daily lives.

After a short dialogue with Yumiko, I realized that Yokoyama was well aware that I was playing with all of the energy I had. What he was trying hard to communicate to me was that with proper breath control and the right frame of mind, not only would I have more energy for shakuhachi, but also much more vitality for life.

Yokoyama went on to explain that I should blow ro every day for ten minutes. Just ro, before any other practice. I was beginning to realize that the mastering of shakuhachi was in one tone, one perfect note, not in how many pieces you knew or how dexterous you were.

Yokoyama then handed me my first piece, called "Honshirabe," which he said was often used as a warmup or a prelude to a main piece. It was the first one I'd learned when I started with Sasaki. I wasn't disappointed though.

The music was written in Japanese *katakana,* a writing system that's read from right to left, down and up. He asked me to play it. Feeling less confident this time than during my temple performance, I began.

A third of the way through it, I realized I was definitely not lost in the music. I was aware of Yokoyama, the audience behind me, a car passing outside, Yumiko at my side, and, most of all, myself. My volume of air was spent before the end of each phrase. I was nervous. I had heard that even great players couldn't give their best in front of this master. The piece ended, and I felt deflated. I heard Yumiko telling him that I was nervous. He replied that nervousness was something I must overcome alone. It's only Ray-san that is concerned about his performance. He must become aware of this and find out why.

It was true. I alone was the self-consumer of my own nervousness.

"Please play it again, Ray-san."

I paused until the sound of a police car with its sirens blared past. The interruption grounded me back into the real world of ordinary people, and I realized that sitting across from me was a very nice gentleman—a person who was going to help me learn to play this flute. The whole room seemed to relax. I played well.

Yokoyama didn't ask the others for their opinions but gave me his. Some of the notes, he said, were too sharp. He told me that I must build up my ki energy. He said I should memorize all the pieces he taught me so that when we played together I could watch him carefully and not have to look at the music.

"You should take the pieces beyond memory," he said. "Then there is the possibility of the inception of something spiritual, Ray-san.

"Please play it again," Yokoyama said.

This time we played in unison. The gravity of his first note startled me, and by the second line I couldn't hear myself. I watched his fingers and head movements intently. Where each of my notes ended abruptly, his finished in perfect pitch and were barely audible, the effect like the final stroke of a calligrapher's brush.

I left at 9:30 PM. Stepping out into the cold December night air, I felt elated. I walked with Yumiko back to the station. She had enjoyed herself and said she wouldn't mind coming every week. Tony was still in the same position, sucking and blowing. A couple of drunks, filled with daring, were wobbling and swaying quite close to him and attempting to prop each other up.

Still buzzing from the lesson, I didn't stop to talk, but decided to buy a hot tea from a nearby vending machine and just sit on the wall across from him and watch. Every now and then a crowd gathered and waited until his two-note tune had concluded, then applauded loudly and threw down some coins. Tony paid little attention to the goings on around him; he just bowed west, then north, then east.

杉
風
之 Chapter Eleven
調 Listening to Incense

The fragrance wafting from the cemetery wasn't Japanese, but I was familiar with the aroma. It reminded me of our time spent in China. I followed the scent through the beautifully landscaped temple gardens of Zuisenji towards the cemetery.

The Zuisenji Temple is tucked away in one of the secluded valleys of the ancient capital city of Kamakura. I'd come here on this day to sit quietly for a couple of hours before visiting my favorite café, called Fue.

For people interested in playing or collecting flutes, Fue was the café to visit. The walls were covered with wind instruments from all over the world, and patrons were welcome to take down the instruments and play them. The shakuhachi on display was cracked and useless, but whenever I visited, the owner brought out a better one from storage for me to play. I often made the two-hour trip to Kamakura to visit the café and perform impromptu concerts.

Nearing the gate of the temple's cemetery, I saw a woman standing in front of a gravestone. Incense smoke swirled about her. She turned and walked towards the gate, moving with incredible elegance and lightness. We greeted each other and commented on the beauty of the spring day.

She wore the dark clothes of mourning. Although elderly, her hair was still black with only a slight streak of gray. It was beautifully held up with a silver clasp. There was a sensitive and cultured look about her, serenity in her manner and posture. I explained, in my halting Japanese, that I had followed the smell of the incense and that it had reminded me of another place and time.

"Smells do that. They can release the smallest, forgotten memory," she said, in near-perfect English. "Are you interested in incense?" Her confident way of speaking surprised me. She lacked the familiar submissive coyness that I'd become accustomed to in so many Japanese women.

"Well, yes, I am, but only to the extent that when I travel I like to collect different types."

We walked slowly into the heart of the garden.

"The incense you can smell is Chinese."

"Yes, I thought it was," I said.

"My husband was from China. He passed away one year ago today. This is the anniversary of his death."

"Oh! I'm sorry to disturb you," I said.

"No, no. It's a pleasure to talk to someone who appreciates 'listening to incense.'"

It was the first time that I'd heard that expression and told her so.

"It comes from *kohdo*. *Koh* means incense, and kohdo is the appreciation of incense," she explained.

We came to a raised long flat stone, which nature had chiseled into a perfect seat. After we had paused to admire it, she suggested we sit down.

I introduced myself, and she replied that her name was Mrs. Chen. With the sun gently warming us, I asked her if she had studied kohdo.

"I wouldn't say that I studied it, but it was always there in my youth. My mother burned it daily ever since I can remember, and taught me all that she knew. She would ask me each day which type of incense was burning. It made my nose quite sensitive. By the time I entered my teenage years, I was able to distinguish the delicate differences of aromas. Incense has quite an interesting history, you know."

I urged her to tell me all about it. She smiled and whisked me back into the sixth century, telling me of the arrival of Buddhism from China and the consequent arrival of incense.

"The purifying smoke and fragrance of the incense have always been an important part of all Buddhist rituals. We Japanese believe that the fragrance will summon the Buddha within us, and that the smoke of the incense will carry our prayers to heaven.

"Not surprisingly," she continued, "it was the nobility of Japan who first started using incense for nonreligious purposes. They started developing subtle new fragrances and searched for rare types of aromatic woods. They cleverly began scenting their clothes and homes with it, and even invented a game called *kumiko,* where several kinds of incense were burned and people gathered to enjoy the scents and see who could correctly guess the different fragrances."

Noticing a young mother and child coming towards us, Mrs. Chen paused for a moment. The child was dressed like a little doll, her downy hair tied up in two bows. She was hanging onto her mother's hand, her little legs wobbling and collapsing every few steps. Mrs. Chen smiled affectionately as they passed us.

"There are so many different types of incense. Do you have a particular favorite, Ray-san?"

"Yes, I've always liked the spicy scent of sandalwood," I replied.

"Yes, it has a wonderful fragrance, doesn't it? It's been used in religious ceremonies in the East for centuries. My husband used to say to me that incense allowed him to unwind from the pressures of daily life and that it somehow brought moments of peace. Have you heard of *koboku,* Ray-san?"

"No, I haven't. What is it?"

"Koboku means aromatic wood and comes from fallen trees that have been buried in tropical forests for hundreds of years. The resin within the wood becomes thick and hard, and when smoldered on hot embers, has an exquisite fragrance. My husband collected many rare and expensive types of koboku over the years."

Mrs. Chen said her favorite wood was called *jinkoh,* adding that she burned this at home on her family altar. She told me its aroma was comforting because the fragrance made her feel as if her husband were in the room with her.

I encouraged her to tell me more about Mr. Chen. She fondly went on to talk about his interest in calligraphy and how every day of his retired life, which had been twenty years until his death, he copied three hundred and sixty kanji, or Japanese characters, of the Heart Sutra, a sermon attributed to Buddha. She reminded me of part of it: "All is emptiness, and emptiness is form."

She went on to tell me that her husband was in perfect health six months before he died. He was eighty-five years old and still active in gardening and walking. Then one day, he missed the chair he was going to sit on and severely injured his back.

It was unusual and refreshing to experience such openness from a Japanese woman. I was glad that she felt comfortable with me and wanted to talk. She said she had been a very traditional Japanese wife and had devoted herself completely to her husband and son. Her husband had left Shanghai and come to Japan after the Second World War as a businessman in his late twenties. She said that he was a creative and farsighted person. It wasn't long before he established his own International Trading Company in Tokyo. Mrs. Chen was recruited by him because of her exceptional English skills, and she quickly became his coordinating assistant for all overseas customers. Two years later they married.

"It wasn't easy," she said, telling me that her parents would not give their consent. Her family was wealthy and had expected their daughter to marry within their social circle.

"There were many wasted years before my husband was accepted. One must follow the heart regardless of the consequences. It took great courage from both of us," she said.

Mrs. Chen was brought up at a time when it was common to have an *o'miai,* or arranged marriage. Marriage was viewed only as an alliance between families. Love marriages were virtually nonexistent; in fact, love was looked upon as a definite disadvantage to the union. It wasn't until the late fifties that men and women began to form personal relationships and choose their own partners.

Dianne occasionally told me about students of hers who were going through the o'miai process of meeting possible partners. O'miai literally means "To see and to meet." Before the candidates meet, they are each given the other's personal résumé by a matchmaker, or *nakodo*. For women, it is advantageous to include domestic abilities, such as cooking, sewing, and any accomplishments in the traditional arts, like calligraphy, tea ceremony, or Japanese dance. For men, it is important to explain future prospects and salary. If both résumés are accepted, the nakodo will then bring the candidates together. If the couple like each other, then they are free to arrange further meetings. When Dianne asked her students why they were considering this method, they either declared that it was their parents' wish or that they simply hadn't met anyone suitable and feared being "left on the shelf." They said they didn't want to end up as stale "Christmas cake," unwanted after the twenty-fifth.

Mrs. Chen asked me the purpose of my visit to Japan. When I told her that I was living here with my wife and was studying shakuhachi, her face lit up. I briefly explained how I'd heard a flute playing in the garden at a Zen retreat and how I met with the old komuso monk, and ultimately became a student of Yokoyama. She seemed delighted, almost thrilled, with my story. She said she remembered seeing komuso monks in the Kyoto area as a young girl.

"You first heard it at a Zen retreat, you say. Are you interested in Zen?" she asked.

"Yes, I've read quite a bit about it over the years and, since being in Japan, I've enjoyed reading about some of the old Zen masters. I find them intriguing, especially the rebels."

"You've read about the Zen masters?" she queried.

"Yes. One of my former shakuhachi teachers encouraged me to read the likes of Bankei, Ryokan, Hakuin, and Ikkyu. I became quite interested in Ikkyu a couple of years ago."

"All admirable men," she said. She paused for a moment, then added, "It would be difficult to find a true master of Zen these days. There is so much business involved in it all now."

"Yes, everything is for sale. Even enlightenment," I said, laughing.

We were silent for a while, then she spoke again. "Would you like to meet the abbot of this temple? I know him well."

"Yes, if it's possible."

"I'm sure it is; he always makes time for his patrons," she said, without irony or sarcasm.

We walked towards the main building.

"Is *abbot* the correct word to use, Ray-san?" she asked.

"Yes it is, but the Japanese word *roshi* has become quite commonly used within Western Zen circles these days," I said.

"Really? Once that title was only used for enlightened Zen masters."

Encircling the main temple of Zuisenji were four small, well-proportioned shrines. The whole area had been restored over the last century and was in perfect balance with the rest of the garden. On our way to the main building, we stopped at one of these shrines. Its shutters were closed, and there was a padlock on the door. Mrs. Chen explained that inside was a wooden statue of the temple founder, and it was only seen by the public once a year. I didn't tell her that, earlier, I had peeped through a crack in the wall.

We entered the administration building, and Mrs. Chen called out to announce our presence. A young man in his twenties, dressed in a gray samue, soon appeared. His head was completely shaven and looked as if it had been polished. There was a polite exchange, and then he disappeared. Two minutes later the abbot appeared, also bald and dressed in a gray samue. After what seemed like an eternity of greetings and countless bows between them, Mrs. Chen introduced me and proudly told the abbot that I was a shakuhachi student, studying with one of the great masters. He turned to face me and bowed politely. I returned the bow.

We were ushered into a small tatami room and asked to make ourselves comfortable. The only piece of furniture was the requisite low lacquered table, a ceramic vase, and a wall scroll. Mrs. Chen knelt in front of the table in seiza with her legs under her. I did the same, then saw the abbot sit in zazen and changed my position so my legs were crossed. The younger man brought tea and poured three cups. We sat quietly for a moment, pondering the green liquid. Mrs. Chen picked up her cup and lightly held it, admiring the craftsmanship and rough texture.

The abbot spoke first.

"Is this your first visit to Kamakura, Ray-san?" His Japanese was slow and quite easy to follow. I answered in English, and Mrs. Chen translated.

"No, Sensei, but this is my first visit to Zuisenji. It's incredibly beautiful. How old is the original temple site?"

"It was founded in 1327, six years before the end of the Kamakura period, by a monk called Soshi. We have a very old image of the monk in one of the shrines, but we only show it once a year. It's a national treasure, you see," he said.

Silence filled the room for a few moments, then Mrs. Chen shared some polite conversation with the abbot. Hearing the sound of the words, but not really listening, I glanced around and thought of something Mrs. Chen had mentioned to me earlier.

She told me of the fantastic sums of money that it cost for the deceased to be given a posthumous Buddhist name and to have a memorial stone placed within the temple grounds. Zen temples, she said, relied exclusively on donations. I had read that the performing of funeral services was almost the sole preserve of Japanese Buddhism today. It seemed to have suffocated itself in hierarchy and ceremony. Only recently, I had spoken to a group of young people who described Japanese Buddhism as cold and gloomy, reminding them only of death.

What had happened to the examination and investigation of truth and meaningful living? All that was left were words.

I looked up at the scroll on the wall, and a wild-eyed monk stared back at me, looking furious, perhaps at the ridiculous system that was forming around him. I imagined him shouting, "Wake up, fools! This is Zen Buddhism, not Yen Buddhism."

I thought of Ryokan, the Zen mystic and poet who lived in the eighteenth and early nineteenth century. He had shunned temple life and refused all offers of position and status, choosing the life of a recluse. Living in a mountain hermitage, he spent all his time writing poetry and talking with the villagers. There had been many before him who had also turned their backs on status and fortune, disassociating themselves from the ceremonial and material trappings of Zen life.

A story flashed into my mind, and I thought about how it would have made those rebels howl. The story goes that the Devil and his advocate were walking aimlessly along the road, when, suddenly, they came across a man preaching to a crowd. The advocate turned to the Devil and said, "Listen to him. He's telling them he's found truth. Let's get him!"

"No, no, no," replied the Devil, laughing. "Leave him. Let him organize it."

From the monotonous drone of a long sentence, I heard the words "shakuhachi" and "Ray-san." Mrs. Chen and the abbot were both looking at me.

"Yokoyama Katsuya," I answered. There was a puzzled look on their faces. He must have asked one of the other standard questions.

Mrs. Chen bailed me out. "Ray-san first heard shakuhachi at a Zen temple in Shimoda."

"Oh, really. We occasionally have shakuhachi concerts here. Perhaps you'd like to come and perform for us in the future?"

"I would be honored," I replied.

The abbot decided that the meeting was over and thanked us for stopping by.

Mrs. Chen and I made our way to the main gate of the temple. It had been such an exceptional morning that I felt it would be appropriate to ask her if she would allow me to take her to lunch. She thanked me but insisted that I be her guest. She said she had already decided to ask me if I wanted to go to her favorite restaurant.

We drove to the restaurant in Mrs. Chen's car. As we passed through the narrow, winding streets of Kamakura, she asked me if I'd heard of the Buddhist term *en* before. I told her I hadn't.

"En means 'an inevitable connection,' or the reason people are sometimes fated to meet by chance or coincidence. En expresses the existence of relationship. Usually in Japan, relationships are established by a go-between," she explained. "But on rare occasions when we meet someone new, en already exists and can be developed. We have to be extremely careful when making new acquaintances. If en doesn't exist, cause and effect can sometimes take you down a dark path. I feel that en already exists between us," she said.

I had to agree. I felt very much at ease with her.

The restaurant was in a suburban part of Kamakura. She said she only lived ten minutes away, and on warm summer evenings, she and her husband used to walk there together.

The tiny entrance delivered us from the busy street into an intimate environment. It was tranquil and calming, one of those small, elegant restaurants that would be difficult to find without a guide. A woman wearing a kimono greeted us. She seemed to know Mrs. Chen well. She took our coats, then led us to a table that overlooked a Japanese garden. I wondered if this had been Mrs. Chen and her husband's special table.

"This style of restaurant is called *shojin-ryori,* which in English means Zen temple food. I'm afraid they only serve Japanese tofu and vegetable dishes here," she said apologetically.

"That's perfect, Mrs. Chen. I don't usually eat meat."

"How very appropriate that we came here then," she said, looking pleased.

I asked if she wouldn't mind ordering for both of us.

While we waited for our food, she asked me if I had come to Kamakura today for some special reason. She seemed to imply that our meeting was not a coincidence. I explained about my visit to the Fue café and how I had only decided to visit Zuisenji Temple after I arrived at Kamakura Station.

"Thank you, Mrs. Chen, for bringing me here. It's really special," I said. "The restaurant has such a rustic beauty about it."

"Yes, unfortunately there aren't many places like this left. They're all disappearing now to make way for new development."

I looked around the room, admiring the aesthetic properties in color and design. I couldn't see anything from the postmodern world. Everything—the cooking utensils, furniture, decorations, and a ceramic vase with some well-placed flowers—had

132

been fashioned out of natural materials. I thought about how Japan's frenzied Western-style modernization was taking its toll on the country's traditions. This was one place it hadn't found yet.

Mrs. Chen gazed out of the window for a few moments, then looked back at me. "I've enjoyed talking to you about the things that were so close to my husband's heart. It really means a great deal to me to visit this place on the anniversary of his death. Thank you for joining me."

"Thank you for inviting me; I'm glad I listened to the smell of the incense."

"Would you like to see a photograph of my husband, Ray-san?" she offered.

"Yes, I would."

She brought out a few faded snapshots, one of a proud looking elderly man standing with a younger man.

"That's my son, Kenichi," she said, smiling. "I wish you could have met him today. Unfortunately, he is always busy, like most Japanese men of his age. He took over the family business after my husband retired."

The other pictures were of Mrs. Chen and her husband, both smiling. There was another of Mr. Chen holding a calligraphy brush doing his morning Heart Sutra ritual. I studied this one a little longer than the others.

"Would you like to see my husband's work after lunch?" Mrs. Chen asked.

"I would love to, but I feel that I've taken up enough of your time already," I said.

"Not at all; this has been a most pleasant day. It would be no trouble at all, Ray-san," she said, smiling warmly.

"Thank you, Mrs. Chen. Then I'd love to."

The food arrived one dish at a time. An exquisite combination of seasonal vegetables, tofu, miso, and rice was served on plates and dishes with colors that were muted and rough, pleasing to the eye. Our host laid it in front of us as if showing us works of art. Mrs. Chen told me that the Zen Buddhists of earlier centuries had strongly influenced the nation's refined style and presentation of Japanese food. Remembering the highly ritualized meals at the Zen retreat, I could clearly see the connections.

"When I was young, my mother and I used to gather wild vegetables in the mountains, and then take them home and cook them," Mrs. Chen said nostalgically.

I couldn't help watching the impeccable way she ate her food, years of form turned into art.

On the way to her home Mrs. Chen said it was unheard of for a Japanese woman to invite a young man home, even if she was in her seventies. But she said she felt that she had known me for many years.

Her home reflected her life with her husband. It was tastefully decorated and had many pieces of fine Chinese art and furniture in the living room. The kitchen was more Western in style, with four wooden chairs and a large oak table. After showing me the living room and lighting a stick of incense on the family altar, she asked me to make myself comfortable at the kitchen table while she made tea.

"This is where my husband sat every morning at 5:30," she said. "Never missed a day."

Her husband's brushes, ink stick, and slate ink stone were still on the table as if they had just been used that morning. She picked up the coal black ink stick; it looked like a worn-down block of sealing wax.

"Every morning before he started his day he would pour a little water on to the ink stone and rub the stick slowly against the stone, still rubbing well after the ink was ready. He said that the preparation stilled his mind."

After serving tea, she left the room, then returned a couple of minutes later carrying some of her husband's calligraphy. She carefully laid the sheets of rice paper on the table in front of me.

"We call Japanese calligraphy *shodo,* the 'way of writing,'" she said.

I stared at a large white sheet of handmade paper, then followed the continuous dance of Chinese characters, not understanding the writing but still reading the characters downwards from right to left. Shakuhachi music was written in the same way, so I was familiar with this way of reading.

Shodo requires years of practice before true freedom of expression can be attained. I knew very little of that true freedom in art, but sensed I was looking at it in Mr. Chen's work.

"They're wonderful. He must have had such spirit and discipline," I said.

"Yes. He was a true master of shodo. Very few people have seen his work. This was the last one he did. I'm going to have it framed," she said, touching the paper gently. She put it aside and showed me the others. "These were the last few he did before he died." Sorting through them, she selected one that she liked.

"I would like you to have this, Ray-san."

I was surprised and protested, saying that I couldn't possibly take it. She insisted, saying that a piece of her husband's spirit would go with me.

"He would like that," she said. "And it will remind you of this day."

杉
風
之
調

Chapter Twelve
Gaijin Komuso

Above the din of the Broadway shopping arcade, I heard a jubilant cry. "Hey! Ray-san, Ray!"

I turned to find Two-Note Tony, his huge frame emerging from the automatic sliding doors of McDonald's.

He said he'd been celebrating. "I've just had the double burger special twice," he said, unsightly traces of his meal still on his chin. "Burnt me bleedin' mouth on the apple pie."

"Sue the bastards," I joked, trying to get him going. "What've you been celebrating, Tony?"

"Had a good night tonight, Ray. Made twenty thousand yen in change. Not bad, eh?"

"No way!" I said, "That's about one hundred and eighty dollars! What'd you make on a bad day, then?"

Rubbing his chin thoughtfully while spreading the traces of mayonnaise into his stubble, he said, "Anywhere from eight to twelve thousand yen. Why don't you try it, Ray? You could probably make the same as me and it definitely beats teaching!"

I walked the rest of the way home thinking about what he said. After a horrendous train journey across the city and a mind-numbing English class with a group of disinterested engineers — just about anything would beat teaching. I had just about had it with teaching English. If it wasn't for the shakuhachi, I'd be the one pushing to leave Japan.

When I arrived home from the station, Dianne was watching sumo wrestling on television. She told me that Hokutoumi had just brought down the huge Hawaiian Konishiki. There was one more fight to go, between Chiyonofuji and Onokuni. With me still standing in my jacket and gripping my bag, we both watched as the grand champion threw Onokuni to the ground.

"Guess how much Two-Note earned tonight, Dianne."

"I don't know. Fifteen hundred, two thousand yen?"

"No. Twenty thousand yen!"

"What! And all this time we've felt sorry for him. That's about a hundred and eighty bucks. Ninety dollars a bloody note," she said, laughing hysterically at her ridiculous calculation.

"Yeah!" I said. "Just think what he could earn if he was able to play the full chromatic scale!"

"Why don't you try it, Ray? It'd be a laugh, wouldn't it? And just think of the experience and practice you'd get."

"Yeah, it'd be a laugh for the audience," I said. "No, I couldn't do it."

"Why not? You play at the temple most days. What's the difference?"

"The difference is that I have permission and, anyway, I don't play for money, do I? Look at the hassle Tony gets all the time. Anyway, where would I play?"

Over the next few weeks I kept thinking about whether I could do the "street musician thing" or not. It would be a way of practicing more, and I could make some money by the sounds of it. But there was no getting away from the fact that I had a problem with the idea of being a street musician. I couldn't deny that I'd walked past many street performers and assumed that they were down on their luck, when maybe they'd actually chosen that lifestyle. The fact that the komuso monks were street musicians did help make the idea more appealing. Only they had played for bowls of rice—I needed yen.

For the Christmas and New Year's holiday, Dianne and I decided to go to the nearby resort town of Atami on the Izu Peninsula. One of Dianne's students generously offered us the use of his holiday condominium, saying it was a lovely place. We jumped at the chance to get out of the city.

The condo was a great switch from our place in Tokyo. It was like a proper apartment, with lots of rooms, a real kitchen, and a bathroom with natural hot spring water piped into it. We were located right on the waterfront with an unobstructed view of the ocean.

Apart from the town's famous hot springs, the other main attractions were the nearby hills and hiking areas with views that stretched as far as Mount Fuji and the scenic area of Hakone and beyond.

Each day Dianne and I left the town and explored the surrounding countryside. It was revitalizing to walk along the trails and through wooded areas. On Christmas morning we climbed more than two thousand feet up to the Atami Pass, found a warm spot in the sun, and ate a rather unseasonal Christmas lunch of brown rice and Japanese vegetables.

The weather was warmer than usual, and the sky was unbelievably clear. We could see Oshima, an active volcano, rising directly from the sea. The view was spectacular. The only sound was the occasional call of a Japanese nightingale.

With Christmas lunch over, we continued to a higher elevation, hoping to glimpse the most famous of all volcanoes, the majestic Mount Fuji.

I had brought my flute to Atami with the hope of getting in some practice, but as usual, it was difficult to play indoors without disturbing the surrounding neighbors.

"Just go and stand somewhere on the waterfront and play," Dianne suggested.

"No way, there's too many people around."

"They'd probably love it," she said. "Anyway, what's the worst thing that could happen?"

"I could be arrested! Or worse, I could die of embarrassment."

"If the police come, just say you're a gaijin komuso, and this is your religious practice!"

"Very funny, Dianne! If you think it's so easy, you come and stand next to me!"

"I'll watch you from the balcony through the binoculars."

"That's brave of you."

"Don't be such a coward, Ray. This would be an excellent place to try busking. You'll never have a better chance."

She was right. It would be a good place, but did I have the nerve?

I walked casually along the promenade, flute in hand, telling myself that I wasn't looking for a good performance spot, but just a place to practice quietly. There were quite a few people about, sauntering along the waterfront. Many of the women were dressed in beautiful kimonos, their husbands or companions in smart suits. Some men and women wore the hotel *yukata,* or cotton kimono, with a short, thick overjacket on top. Seeing all these people graciously strolling along put me in a good mood. With no other foreigners around, I felt as if I was really in Japan.

I reached an unusual-looking bronze statue of a young woman down on her knees. Standing over her, poised as if about to strike her, was a man dressed in a soldier's uniform. A plaque mounted beneath the statue was written in kanji. I studied it for a few moments, hoping to spot some of the Japanese characters that I had memorized. A woman approached, saw me struggling, and asked if I could read the characters. I told her that I couldn't and then, taking advantage of her language skills, asked if she could tell me what it said. Without reading the plaque, she explained why the man was angry.

"The man is striking his fiancée in a fit of rage," she said. "The young woman has told the soldier that she loves him but must break off their engagement because she has been promised by her parents to a wealthy, more suitable man. The young lady, apparently sad, but impressed by the other man's wealth, complies with her parents' wishes. The soldier," she said, pointing to the statue of the man, "is of low rank and feels deeply bitter and hurt at his fiancée's cruel betrayal. It's a very famous story in Japan," she concluded. Stepping back, she removed her camera from her bag and clicked a photograph of the sad couple.

"The story goes," she continued, "that after leaving the army, the soldier found a job as a lowly clerk. He worked so hard that he became very wealthy in his own right and eventually bought up the company he worked for. The woman renewed her interest in him, but although he still loved her, he wouldn't have anything to do with her."

As she walked off, several people came up and had their photograph taken next to the statue. I decided to stay and sit on the wall for a while, watching the people coming and going. I thought it would be a great place to play the flute. I sat there for ages, not really seeing the people but imagining myself playing. Several times I started to unwrap the flute, then some people would come by and I'd lose my nerve and quickly cover it up. Deep down, I really wanted to play. Breathing deeply, I finally got the thing completely out of its bag and began inspecting it like I hadn't seen it before.

I held it firmly around the neck, and peering down the barrel, tried to warm the bamboo with my hands. At that moment, a group of people came by, saw the flute, and started saying, "Shakuhachi, shakuhachi," to one another.

"Dozo, dozo. Please play. Dozo," one of the men said, smiling.

The women started encouraging me with little pleading claps of their hands. I nonchalantly agreed, and before I could change my mind, blew a few warm up notes and began to play a well-known song called "Kojo no Tsuki" or "Moon Over the Castle." After the first two notes, there was a burst of applause that made me think that perhaps that was all that was needed, but I continued, and by the end of the song there was a frantic clicking of cameras and a chorus of "Sugoi, sugoi!" I'd done it! They thanked me, asked for my address so that they could send photographs, bowed, and walked away chattering about the foreigner.

I buzzed with excitement. More people in the distance came towards me. I wanted to play again, so I proceeded confidently into another popular folk song. A group of people stopped, listened to the song, then applauded and moved on.

In a state of euphoria and brimming with confidence, I quickly unfolded some of my sheet music, put it on the floor, and dropped a handful of coins on top of it. I hoped Dianne had the binoculars on me now. Before I lost my nerve, I started playing again. Within moments there was a group of people standing around me, listening and commenting on my ability.

"He must have played a long time."

"He's very good, isn't he?"

"I wonder what country he's from?"

"He's moving his head well. He must have played a while."

A woman stepped forward out of the group and dropped a handful of coins onto the music sheet. Someone else followed.

Then another, and another, until all of them had placed some coins down. I was cringing and feeling excited at the same time. What should I do? I bowed up and down, bobbing slightly and rhythmically without stopping the music. I must have looked ridiculous, like some great long-billed bird. They moved on. More people approached.

I started playing the same song. This time the group didn't stop. As they passed, they gestured a clap only. The next group did the same, but one of the well-dressed older women stopped about ten feet past me, leaned on her walking stick, and listened. After a couple of minutes she instructed a young man from the group to walk back and put some money down. He approached, opened his wallet, pulled out the equivalent of about twenty dollars, and placed it on the music sheet. With a little bow, he thanked me and said his mother appreciated that I'd taken the time to study shakuhachi, one of Japan's dying arts. "It has made my mother very happy to hear it today."

I had never expected such interest.

Another group was approaching in the distance.

When we returned to Tokyo, Dianne and I started thinking about places where I could play. We both agreed that it had to be somewhere that wasn't noisy and most important, where it wasn't polluted. This limited my choices considerably, and in truth, I really didn't want to play on a street at all. What I wanted was somewhere like Arai Yakushi Temple, but with people who wouldn't recognize me. Perhaps a popular Japanese tourist spot, where people came and went all the time. Resorts like Atami were great, but too far away.

A place called Mount Takeo, a couple of hours west of Tokyo, kept coming to mind. It was an area that Dianne and I regularly visited to hike, breathe fresh air, and get away from the city. Dianne said it would be the perfect place for shakuhachi, but I kept resisting because I thought, with it being a protected park area, that I'd get told to move on by the authorities.

Dianne finally insisted that we go there on the following Saturday.

We arrived early in the morning. It was a brilliant January day with blue skies and cold, dry air. The parking lot was almost full, and people were lined up for the cable car and chair lift. On foot it was an exhilarating two-hour hike to the summit. If you stuck to the tourist route, you passed through a cluster of shrines and temples on the way. The buildings were evenly spaced and connected by well-trodden footpaths lined with momiji and ginkgo trees and the occasional massive cedar. On clear days, people hiked from the temples to the summit, hoping for a good view of Mount Fuji. This was a magnificent area, and the atmosphere was perfect for shakuhachi. My only concern was that monks and temple officials regularly walked to an administration building on the summit. Would they object? Would my presence offend or disturb anyone? We decided to return the next day to find out.

We were up by 6:00 AM. Dianne busily packed us a picnic lunch and said that she would hang around with me for the first hour or so once we were on the mountain. Then, when I felt confident, she would go off hiking and return at noon to see how I was doing. The mountain was quiet when we arrived, but soon would be overflowing with people once the cable car and chair lift started operating.

We hiked to an area we'd found on the previous day, a good spot on the main path that connected two temples. There was a huge cedar tree at the side of the path. I could stand under it and not impede the flow of the hundreds of amblers. Taking a deep breath, I set up my music stand in front of me like a protective wall, then began quietly playing. Dianne found a place to sit, made herself comfortable, and then took a couple of photographs of me.

The first people to stop were a monk and a temple official. Well, this was it: either the start of a new career or a long hike down the mountain. They listened for a while. I got the impression that they were waiting for me to stop so that they could ask me to clear off. I played on, cringing inside, wishing they'd go away. To my surprise, that's just what they did, but before they left the monk said in broken English, "Very good . . . you play."

Once they were out of sight, and with that major hurdle overcome, I placed one of my music sheets on the ground in front of me, threw a few coins on to it, and feeling more relaxed, proceeded to play. The response was fantastic. People stopped to chat and take pictures. Some sat on the bank opposite to listen. People who had passed by on their way up to the summit stopped on their way back down and offered me drinks and snacks. It was the most incredible day.

I made over three hundred and fifty dollars in the six hours I was there. That night, on the way home, we stopped off at our favorite sushi restaurant for a celebration dinner.

From then on, weather permitting, I spent most of my weekends playing on Mount Takeo.

I was pretty sure now that I could make almost as much money busking as I did teaching, but I wondered whether I'd spoil my relationship with shakuhachi by playing too much. Dianne thought that this was impossible and said it was the teaching that would spoil my relationship with shakuhachi, if anything! She thought the busking idea was brilliant and immediately said I should give up my company classes altogether and take a chance.

A month later, confident about my finances, I resigned from my full-time teaching job with four months left on my working visa. Visas were valid for one year and only available if you had the proper sponsorship from a recognized Japanese company. I had two choices once mine expired, either get a ninety-day tourist visa, which would mean doing a turnaround to Korea each time it expired, or, jump through hoops and apply for the almost-impossible-to-get cultural visa. I had heard of people receiving this type of visa for some of the martial and other traditional arts, but I hadn't met anyone who'd been given one to study shakuhachi.

After discussing my options with Dianne, I asked my translator friend Yumiko to call immigration, state my case, and find out exactly what I needed to do. The results of this call weren't very promising. Yumiko told me that the person she'd spoken to had said it was a very difficult visa to obtain as so many requirements had to be met. Just to be considered, I'd need to produce a letter of reference from an independent guarantor who must be a Japanese male citizen. The guarantor, in turn, would have to show his last two years of tax receipts and promise to take full responsibility for any debts I might incur or trouble I might cause while on Japanese soil. I'd need a letter from a recognized shakuhachi master, outlining in minute detail my curriculum, lesson schedule, and fees. I'd need to show all my educational certification and all my Japanese tax receipts, as well as all my earned income for the last two years. I'd also have to show financial proof that I could support myself without working, which would mean producing bank statements and evidence of other sources of income. In addition, I'd have to outline all my living expenses, such as rent, bills, and other overheads in Japan. Amazed at this list, I joked to Yumiko that perhaps I might need to supply a blood and urine sample as well.

"No," she said seriously. "That won't be necessary in this case, Ray-san."

I was now faced with a true test of my commitment to shakuhachi. With four months to collect all the paperwork together, I decided optimistically to give it a try.

Collecting all the necessary statements, certificates, and tax receipts was a horrendous task. Yumiko asked Yokoyama if he would be willing to sponsor me and explained what would be required of him. He said he would be more than pleased to help.

Dianne arranged an interview for me with one of her company clients. He liked me, liked what I was attempting to do, and agreed to be my guarantor.

On the appointed day, accompanied by my guarantor and Dianne, we went to the immigration office in Otamachi. With my shakuhachi laid out on the desk along with all my paperwork, in triplicate, we humbly smiled, nodded, and looked serious when serious looked like it was needed. Then we listened as my generous guarantor did most of the talking. The officer, periodically shaking his head, sucked through his teeth and shuffled through my papers, looking down, looking up, looking at me, then looking at Dianne. Naturally, I was one minor piece of information short. I said I could have the missing piece here by tomorrow morning, first thing.

One month later I received a postcard in the mail saying that my guarantor and I must attend an interview with a senior immigration officer.

The officer wasn't in a good mood when I arrived that morning, and he grilled me for fifteen minutes without looking directly at me once. Staring at my papers, he shook his head. It didn't look promising. I had been answering his questions in my survival Japanese. I decided to take a chance and state my case in English.

"May I speak frankly, Sensei?" He didn't say anything, so I continued. "I'm not here in Japan just to take advantage of the system. I'm not here just to make money." At this point he looked directly at me. "I really am dedicated and serious about studying

149

shakuhachi. I've been studying diligently for several years, and my goal is to become the best player I can possibly be."

The Japanese love words like *dedicated, serious,* and *diligent;* they love the word *goal,* too.

He stood up, left the room, and came back ten minutes later, whereupon he handed me my passport and said, "Please study hard. I expect a report from your Sensei every three months, delivered by you in person." He bowed and said good day.

Chapter Thirteen
Impermanence

With the arrival of spring comes a time of celebration in Japan. *Hanami,* the annual custom of cherry blossom viewing, in Tokyo, takes place in early April. The viewing custom probably goes as far back as the Buddhist ceremonies among the court nobles of the twelfth century, but didn't gain widespread popularity until the seventeenth century.

In Japan, there is a collective interest in blossom viewing, the falling blossoms often used as a metaphor for impermanence, the evanescence of life. I was frequently reminded by the Japanese that, as a foreigner, I would never be able to fully understand the Japanese aesthetic appreciation of hanami. They weren't wrong about that—for most, the period from the sight of the first flower to the delicate falling of the petals appeared to be one long drinking binge.

Ueno Park is one of the most popular areas in Tokyo to view cherry blossoms. Thousands visit each year at this time. In the early afternoon, you can see the newly hired company recruits, assigned to the job of reserving spaces under various cherry trees, dozing on huge blue ground sheets. Their colleagues will show up after work laden with sake, beer, and food. By early evening there are hundreds of revelers sitting in large circles. Literally covering the ground, these otherwise orderly people let loose and celebrate under the hanging boughs of the ancient blossom trees.

The festival attracts many foreign street musicians, and I decided that this year I wanted to be among them, playing several hours a day for each of the event's seven days.

I visited the park the day before the festival began and walked around searching out a good spot for the following day. There weren't many people around. The boardwalk was lined from end to end with cherry trees. The buds were just beginning to open, offering a delicate hint of pale pink as far as the eye could see. Old-fashioned lanterns strung around the area gave the place a feeling of old Japan. I found a location near a streetlight about midway along the path and hoped it wasn't already taken. It seemed as good a place as any.

I unwrapped the flute and slipped it from its bag, then began to play quietly. Two children walking their dog were startled into silence when they saw me. For a few seconds they were as still as little statues. There was an air of curiosity and caution about them that quickly turned to smiles and giggles when I said good morning to them in English.

Extra police had been assigned to the park in readiness for the merrymaking that would soon take place. A police officer, cycling his rounds, was headed in my direction. He stopped, and, straddling his bike, watched me and listened. Was he going to make me move on? The piece finished. I said good morning, to which he responded, "Goodo morning. Sugoi," and then asked what country I was from and who my teacher was. With another sugoi, he smiled, said, "Gambatte," and cycled off.

I decided to play from 3:00 PM until 8:00 PM each day, weather and energy level permitting.

I arrived early in the afternoon on the first day of the festival, found my spot, and relaxed for a while on the grass in the warm sun. The street vendors, many of whom were Israeli, were busy setting up their stalls. A young man had already set up his jewelry table close to where I was going to play. I walked up to him and said hello and told him I'd be playing shakuhachi a few yards away from him this week.

"*Sakahoochi, sakahoochi.* What's this *sakahoochi?*" he asked, rather aggressively, warming up a bit when I explained that it was a Japanese bamboo flute and was no threat to his business.

"This I don't mind, my friend," he said. "Which country you from?"

"England," I said.

"Ah, an Englishman. I'm from Israel." He thrust his hand out. "I'm Avi, seller of little shaking insects!" he pushed one into my hand. The rubber beetle was mounted in a walnut-shaped box and quivered quite realistically.

"Pleased to meet you, Avi. I'm Ray."

"Hey! Maybe we can watch out for each other when it really gets rocking tonight. You can look after my stall for me sometimes, yeah? We can help each other?"

"Yeah, sure," I said, "and you can play 'sakahoochi' for me!"

There was a fairground atmosphere in the air, the workers setting up, the crowds yet to come. I liked it.

A man with fair, shoulder-length wavy hair stopped by at Avi's table and shook his hand. The man was dressed in a top hat, well-worn tails, and a white shirt. Under one arm he carried a fold-up table and a large blue and pink striped bag. After a minute, Avi pointed over at me. Leaving his belongings, the long-haired man walked over, and, in that easy American way, asked me how I was doing, mentioning that he hadn't seen me around before.

There was a sort of oddball, "astrotraveler" manner about him. He asked me a couple of questions about the flute, said, "Far out, man!" a few times, and then told me that he was a magician known as the "The Penguin" on the buskers' circuit. He said he performed on the streets of Europe and the States and spent his winters hanging out in Pushkar, India. I said that I had spent a lot of time in Dharamsala in the north. He knew the area well and said he'd performed there for the Dalai Lama once, adding that a little kid monk had volunteered to be his assistant.

"What a trip that was, man," he said, drifting off into another place.

The Penguin only "worked" Japan in the blossom season, saying that without the language, it wasn't worth staying longer. His act had a lot of banter in it and needed audience participation. This, he said, was tough in Japan because the people were too shy to join in. They also didn't like to step up and put money in the hat at the end of the show.

As he turned to leave, he said wistfully, "I need a ringer, man, someone to show the way."

The Japanese call this method of drawing people out *sakura,* the same word that's used for "cherry blossom," the sakura in this case being elusive. Once a person gathered the courage to step forward and give money, others, usually feeling a little obliged, tended to follow suit. Such is the power of the group.

The Penguin wasn't the only strange sight I was to encounter that day.

"Yer dinna have a wee bit a toilet paper, do yah by any chance, mate?"

Standing in front of me, like a vision, was a Scottish piper in full regalia, right down to the dagger in the sock.

"No, mate. I've got some tissue paper though. Will that do?" I rummaged through my bag and pulled out one of those tiny packets of tissues that are handed out free at all the train stations.

"Aye, that'll do nicely," he said, rushing off in the direction of the toilets with his kilt swinging around him.

A few minutes later he was back, and, without preamble, in a broad Glasweigeon accent, said, "If I'd been wearing me trrrousers, a woulda'na made it." We both laughed, and then, nodding towards my flute, he said, "Do yer mek much money with that wee thing?" I told him I did all right. He said he'd made enough money with the pipes over the years to buy a "wee hoose" in a good area of Edinburgh.

He asked if I'd worked here before, and I replied that it was my first time.

"A' did'nee think soo. Where do yer usually play?"

I told him that the shakuhachi was a Zen flute, so I normally only played around temple areas outside of the city.

"Do yer get much trrrouble?"

I told him no, not much.

"If ya did, I bet you could give someone a nice wee clobber with that."

I asked him if he had much trouble.

"Och, no. Are you kiddin'? Who the hell would come near me dressed like this?"

We introduced ourselves, and Jock explained that, like most performers here, he was on a three-month tourist visa, following the "blossom mania" circuit from south to north.

He warned me that the festival got pretty crazy once the drink took hold, and said I should keep my faculties about me.

"Never touch the drrrink when yer werking. Never leave much money on the grroond. If there is the slightest bother, walk away. Be polite and respectful, ne'er forget that, mate, and don't be mouthy with the *yakuza*—they can be bastards. You can see them comin'. They're the ones who dress like 'I'm a hard man, I'm a gangster.' They walk aroond in packs—bit risky tacklin' that many. If there were only two or three o' them, they'd be nee bother." I think he was serious.

Because of the loudness of Jock's instrument, he didn't play along the boardwalk but used a spot farther along, in a large, open area of the park well away from the other musicians, thank goodness. The Japanese loved his act and saw him as a kind of

Scottish samurai. I'm sure he would have called their samurai "a bunch o' wee pufftas."

Another loud performer at the festival was Tokyo Ted, whom I'd spoken to many times over the years. He did a one-man band show and performed all over the city. His act lasted about fifteen minutes a set, and he attracted around thirty people to each session. Tokyo Ted, in fact an Australian, had a shaggy, weatherworn look about him. His body was hunched, and his shoulders were rounded, probably because of the large drum he carried on his back, and all the other instruments that were strapped to his body all day.

I watched Ted one night, and after every set, he collected between thirty and a hundred dollars, depending on the time of night. People in his crowd were usually drunk and rowdy, tampering with his equipment, and banging his drum. He had a minder who tried to keep them at bay, but the poor young lad was ineffectual against the sake-confident drunks.

One night I bumped into Ted at Shinjuku Station. He was holding the automatic doors of the train open with the full weight of his body while his minder struggled to load all his equipment into the carriage. We talked, and I asked him where he was living these days.

"Well, mate," he said in his twangy Australian accent. "I'm in your neck of the woods at the moment, dossing down in a classroom across from the Sun Plaza."

I asked him how he had managed that little scam.

"Me mate's an English teacher, isn't he? He's got the key to the school where he works. Nice one, eh?" he said, laughing.

"When I can't stay there I doss down on a mate's floor." I knew what was coming next.

"How big's your apartment, Ray?"

"Not big enough for you, Ted." I replied, laughing.

Dianne came to the park a few of times during the week to take photographs of me and some of the other buskers and to enjoy the cherry blossom scene. I didn't see much of her though, because each time she turned up, Avi roped her into looking after his stall so that he could take a break and get some food.

Amid all of these international performers, there were a few Japanese acts as well. One older woman called Muira-san sang and played on the *shamisen,* a three-stringed Japanese lute that has a small box covered in cat skin. To the untrained ear, the shamisen sounds like a flat banjo. Muira-san went from group to group, playing and singing old Japanese folk songs. She was a sprightly woman with the air of someone much younger, and she performed with great style and grace. After a while, Muira-san and I got to know each other, and at least once a day she came to my spot, where we would play a duet together. A crowd of about thirty people would usually gather to see this dignified lady, dressed in kimono, jamming with the gaijin.

Muira-san said she had played shamisen for many years, and as a young woman she had trained in the traditional arts. I felt privileged when she told me that she really enjoyed our duets.

She revealed that she had been coming to the blossom festival for the last twenty years, but that this was the first time she had ever performed with a foreigner.

Before the last few petals fell that season, Muria-san taught me five new folk songs, patiently singing them line by line until I got them right.

My last night at the park was a beautiful, warm evening. The scent of spring air and blossoms was intoxicating, and amid the drunken festivities the pink lanterns in the trees added an ethereal quality to the already soft pink glow of the night, creating an almost surreal scene.

A steady stream of people stopped and asked the usual questions, wanting to know who my teacher was and how long I'd been playing. "Gambatte," they'd always say, encouraging me on.

I was having my best day ever, monetarily speaking. Audience members were, for the most part, happy and charming, taking my photograph and singing along with the music. A few strange characters tried to annoy me, but with little success. They were drunks mostly, hanging around yelling or trying to speak English. When this happened I would stop playing, and they would eventually move on. But one shady-looking individual kept returning. I wondered if he was a pickpocket looking for business. He'd hang around for quite a while, acting suspiciously, and I could tell he wasn't interested in the music. Each time I saw him, I'd stop playing and make very direct eye contact, then silently wait until he disappeared into the crowd.

The five or six large parties in close proximity to my spot seemed to enjoy the music. The alcohol was having its desired effect, and members of the different groups started calling out requests. As on most nights, the groups gave me cups of sake and plates of food from their picnics, and passed around a hat for me. All the money I made was thrown in my open bag on the ground. People were incredibly generous.

As it grew later in the evening, a crowd of about fifteen people formed a large semicircle in front of me. I guessed that this would be my last song of the evening, so I chose an upbeat number, a folk song that had been popular all week. A few people in the audience were taking pictures, so I walked from side to side so they could get action shots. While I was doing this, I heard and saw the crowd gasp. I immediately stopped playing as someone shouted that my bag had been stolen.

The audience, in disbelief, stood in silence for a moment.

"*Daijobu, daijobu.* Shoganai. It's okay. What's done is done," I said.

One woman, almost in tears, started speaking in Japanese to the people around her. A few others joined in. I again repeated, truthfully, that it was okay, and told them not to worry. I said that I was stupid for being so careless, and that no harm was done. It was only money.

But soon everyone in the crowd opened their wallets and purses. I protested, but all I could do was watch as the scene unfolded. The young woman who had first spoken to the crowd collected the money and handed it to me. She apologized and said that the thief had not been part of the crowd. I thanked them and bowed, then asked if I could play another piece for them.

"Hai! Dozo. Yes, please!" was their unanimous answer.

"What would you like me to play?" I asked.

"Amazing Grace," someone called.

Others gave their agreement. I composed myself. No one moved. There was complete silence around me. Passersby, sensing something special, joined the group. Imagined or real, the air felt charged with the human spirit. The notes drifted into the night air, the breeze carrying them through the darkness.

When I finished the piece, I slowly removed the flute from my mouth. There were a few seconds of silence, then the newcomers began to clap and call out, "Well done, very beautiful." I felt tired. The woman at the front thanked me, and others followed her cue. Seeing I had no bag, she removed what appeared to be a silk blouse from a large shopping bag she was carrying and handed it to me saying, "Dozo, please use this bag for your shakuhachi."

After much bowing, handshaking, and well-wishing, the crowd drifted off into the night.

杉
風
之
調 # Chapter Fourteen
Shakuhachi Marathon

Ahhh! Yes . . . this is the real me, no shadow of conflict, no entanglements of attachment, no separation from bird, beast, or beetle.

That was me on the morning of the fifth day of what was to be a sixty-day, self-imposed *shugyo*.

Shugyo, which means "practice," comes from the word *shugendo,* or the "ascetic path to realization," and describes spiritual exercise or training. It can take any form, just as long as deeply focused discipline is present and ki energy is developed.

My chosen form of practice was to hike up Mount Takeo each day, and, once at the top, play shakuhachi for six hours, then hike back down again. My aspirations weren't so lofty as to become an "awakened one" but simply to increase my physical strength, vastly improve my musical skills, develop ki, and learn more about discipline.

One can hopefully be forgiven for mistaking states of mind, so joyous, so high-spirited, for authentic self-realization. The weekday solitude and silence, combined with hour upon hour of deep breathing, had brought about moments of mindfulness that I could only term as an "oxygen-induced nirvana." Those first four days, although extremely tiring, were incredible. There was no resistance in me. The mid-October weather was glorious, and I was focused and excited about the training and about spending every day on the mountain. Filled with oxygen, a sense of freedom, and an unshakable feeling of confidence, I basked in how great life was and marveled at the beauty of discipline.

By noon on the fifth day, massive black clouds started to build overhead, and by two o'clock it was pouring rain. With this dramatic change in the weather, my "unshakable confidence" teetered, my mindfulness dulled, and my spirit instantly sank into my wet runners. The weather stayed like this for five more days. The mornings became so cold that it was difficult to leave the folds of my flannel sheets and Dianne's warm body. On those days, the chilling reality of what I'd taken on set in, and I spent many a dismal hour wondering whether I could justify this sixty-day act of lunacy, especially as it was going to get even colder. This resistance quickly stirred my ego. *I can't give up, I* must *complete this challenge,* I told myself harshly. *One day at a time. I can stop at any point. I don't* have *to do the full sixty days if I don't want to,* I told myself cunningly. *Think how great I'll feel when I've completed the sixty days,* I told myself seductively.

Protected by the trees from the worst of the rain, I stiffly played on with frozen fingers, cold, wet feet, and a runny nose, while a hundred angry questions formed an endless queue in my head.

Shit! What am I doing up here? It's absolutely ludicrous standing here. Sixty days! And me supposed to be a man of no goals! Why would anyone in his right mind spend his time standing on the side of a mountain in the pissing rain? I could have stayed at home and done my sixty days at my own temple. Prat! It's bloody embarrassing. I'm freezing, my legs are aching, and my back is killing me. I bet I'm the only fool on this mountain today.

By the eleventh day, the wild high and low mood swings started to stabilize along with the weather, and I found myself gaining in physical and mental strength. I began to settle into the rhythm of the challenge with more presence of mind and less focus on the goal of day sixty.

The circumstances that led up to my shugyo came about after a meeting with my first teacher, Yamada-san. We'd kept in touch regularly by telephone since I'd finished studying with him, but this was the first time I'd actually seen him in over three years.

I was invited to perform in a small concert at his studio, which turned out to be an enjoyable reunion. When all the guests left, Yamada and I sat together and talked. He said he was thrilled by my performance and surprised at how far I'd come with the shakuhachi in such a short time. He then asked me how much longer I planned to stay in Japan. I told him that I wasn't sure, maybe another eighteen months or two years, I didn't know. He seemed extremely concerned with my answer.

"Shakuhachi is your forte, Ray-san. You could be a master one day, but to do that you need more time than you have. More time could mean the difference between being a fine flute player, which you already are, and becoming a master. It's up to you, Ray-san." He paused for a moment to pour us both a glass of sake.

"It takes a combination of time and dedication, Ray-san, to master the brush or the sword. Shakuhachi is no different. To reach that level of mastery requires tremendous discipline."

For the next couple of weeks I thought about what Yamada had said. It had been a constant concern and one I had struggled with from the very beginning. I knew it would be difficult to maintain the level I was at if I left, and I knew it would be nearly impossible to further develop my skills outside of Japan. To attain anything like the mastery needed to keep growing without a teacher would mean having to stay at least another three years. I didn't want to do that, and I knew Dianne didn't want to stay that much longer either. We'd already been in Japan for four years as it was.

Around the time of my reunion with Yamada, I had become friends with one of Yokoyama's students, a fellow called Kazu. One evening on the way home from our lesson, I talked to him about my predicament. He listened sympathetically and immediately suggested that I do a shakuhachi shugyo as he himself had once done. He then went on to tell me about Yokoyama's teacher, the late Watazumi.

Watazumi had developed extraordinary power and breath control by practicing vigorous physical disciplines. Apparently, his shugyo involved rising at 3:30 AM every day, hurling a long hardwood pole, called a *jo* stick around his body, and then practicing shakuhachi for several hours. He maintained this shugyo for three thousand consecutive days. Inspired by this old master's practice, Kazu created his own shugyo by playing shakuhachi for two and a half hours every day for two months.

"I couldn't believe how fast my skills accelerated, Ray-san; it was like a year's worth of study in two months," he said.

Impressed by Kazu's advice, I decided the discipline of a shugyo was what I needed and the best way to improve my playing ability within a short time. One week later, with my few private English students temporarily passed over to other teaching friends, I found myself standing under the now-familiar cedar tree on Mount Takeo with fifty-nine days to go!

Each morning in the half-light of dawn I made my way to Nakano Station and waited for the 6:39 AM express train that would take me to the small station below the mountain. Any later than this and I had to stand for an hour in a train packed with university students and office workers. Those lucky enough to get seats slept soundly; even some left standing managed to get a little slumber. But those awake, unable to read for lack of space, rode in a calm, isolated silence. A form of commuter shugyo, I thought.

On cold, dark days, I would see perhaps two or three people all day—on rainy days, none. I made up a few rules that I stuck to: Don't look shabby, keep to the same schedule every day, and don't play for money, but if it comes, fine.

There were some days when I hiked up the mountain with the sole intention of recapturing the highs that I was to occasionally experience during the sixty-days—highs that were unmistakably free of self-centeredness, periods during the long days alone when quietude came naturally and not through absorption or effort. In these moments the same memory-dependent thoughts rose and set in their habitual way, but without interference, without attachment. I could see myself undistorted, exactly as I was programmed to be. One can see many absurd things about oneself while watching old memory reruns. Then again, when there's intense watching, is there anyone there to feel absurd at all?

In late fall Mount Takeo was virtually deserted on weekdays, so it was easy to concentrate all my energy into my practice, mostly undisturbed. But with the weekends came hundreds of pilgrims, hikers, families, and all kinds of groups. Many wanted to make contact, and because I was in such a public spot, I became more sociable, yet I was still able to keep my practice intact.

The visitors who passed by included immaculately turned-out, chattering homemakers with pale, porcelain complexions and bright red lips, schoolchildren on nature rambles, and retired corporate warriors carrying enough equipment to conquer K2. Why did they need ice axes? One day, as I was hiking up to my spot, I saw a man on the trail energetically telling his group where they were positioned by using a hand-held electronic satellite map. The sign nearby read: *Five km Mount Takeo summit.*

Mornings with blue skies brought groups of darling little children from the cable car terminus below. By the time they reached me, their five- and six-year-old legs couldn't keep them in their designated pairs. I'd stop playing and watch as they struggled and staggered past me, battling towards the summit, some with backs bent, hands on knees. They were identically dressed in their school uniforms, and only the color of their hats—blue for boys and pink for girls—was different. The whole scene gave me the impression that these little imps were already preparing for a life of discipline and self-denial.

Two perfectly composed teachers took up the rear, each holding a hand of one sobbing child whose little knees were muddied and grazed—casualties of the tough climb. Seeing me, the teachers came to a halt and pointed, trying to distract the child from the painful memory of her fall. The pink hat lifted, and a little round, tear-stained face with the most beautiful black eyes stared back at me. My foreign face did the trick!

Almost every day at the same time, the same three shaven-headed, black-robed monks would pass me. I'd see them once on their way up to the summit and again on their way down. This was their discipline. They always chanted as they passed and paid little attention to me. They had asked all they wanted to know about me weeks ago at the temple. I promised them I'd go and see them on my last day. I guess they were curious to see if I would complete the sixty days or not. I always stopped playing when I caught sight of them so I could listen to their melodious chanting. On still days, I would hear them coming before I saw them, their chant carrying on the crisp air.

By early November, the temperature dropped and ground frost started to appear in the early mornings. Standing in the cold seemed to shrink body and mind. The winds were the worst. Fingers became numb, making it almost impossible to blow a note. On these occasions, it was rare for a group of women to pass without stopping and holding my freezing hands in theirs, each taking turns and commenting on how cold mine were. This was the height of generosity, the sharing of warm hands with a stranger.

Many of the older people who knew shakuhachi well would stop, talk of the komuso monks, and knowing the tradition, leave fruit, rice balls, sake, and kind words. On weekends, food and cups of sake from vending machines mounted up so much so that I would sometimes take a detour on the way home and give the surplus to the street people at Shinjuku Station in downtown Tokyo.

The train stations around Tokyo were now home to hundreds of homeless people. Some, I'd been told, had broken down mentally or emotionally due to the pressures of their jobs or their home lives. Others had migrated to the city from surrounding prefectures, hoping to be hired by the once-booming construction industry. Over the last year the air had begun to escape from the Japanese economic bubble, and now these construction workers were only exploited for occasional day work. I'd heard that they were organized by the yakuza, or Mafia, to benefit Japanese businesses.

To make my deliveries, I passed through the warren of cardboard box shelters, most of which were well constructed. All looked reasonably clean and tidy. Hard-worn shoes were placed neatly outside each entrance. With a shout of "*Sumi-masen.* Excuse me," an occupant would stick his head out of his box and accept the food and sake graciously, politely apologizing in the Japanese way. I noticed that no matter to whom I gave food and sake, it was always shared with others. I'd seen them form small parties of six or eight people, covering the ground with newspapers, then sitting crossed-legged in a circle. The food and drinks were placed neatly in the center, with their shoes removed and off to the side, never touching the paper.

A couple of weeks into my shugyo, a rather surly old monk, whom I'd seen many times, came by on his way up the mountain and said it was unusual to see me standing here on weekdays.

"You only weekend komuso," he had said without humor.

I explained as best as I could in a mixture of Japanese and English about the sixty-day shugyo. He seemed pleased and commented that it was interesting to see a foreigner take on this kind of difficult komuso training.

"You will put tengai on head?" he asked, miming the action of completely covering his head with an imaginary reed basket hat in the style of the old komuso monks.

"No. I'm sorry, Sensei," I apologized.

He looked disappointed.

"Real komuso put tengai," he scolded, miming the action again.

"I'm sorry, Sensei." More disappointment appeared on his face.

"I 'shugyo' every day . . . mountaintop . . . back!" he boasted.

"Ah, so desu? Is that right?" I said.

"Shugyo make . . . strong *hara,*" he said slapping his belly.

"Ah! So desu ka?" I replied.

Bushido, the code of the warrior, claims that the hara or spiritual center, corresponds with the lower abdomen, and is the focal point of the vital force of human beings.

"You shugyo, have strong spirit," he said, tapping his belly again. "I shugyo every day. Mountaintop, back," he reminded me.

"Ah! So!" I replied again and thanked him for his advice.

He was not wrong. The hike up and down the mountain each day was certainly strengthening my resolve and my body. There were some days when I maintained a fast pace all the way to my spot at the cedar tree, arriving soaked in sweat and breathing deeply. But within one or two minutes my breath had recovered enough to blow a long, even note. I had originally started the fast pace for the first twenty minutes of the hike only, in a desperate attempt to escape the Japanese announcements and the recorded bird music that was played over a speaker system for the pleasure of the cable car passengers.

Sometimes on the way down in the evening I'd call in at a small Zen temple. Within its grounds was the well-known Biwa waterfall. It was used regularly by religious devotees performing *taki-shugyo,* or waterfall training. If you were lucky, you could see a disciple standing under the freezing flow. The ritual took about an hour to complete. They would shower first, then pray and chant mantras. Candles were lit and placed near small statues of Buddha. Finally, with only a thin cloth covering them, these disciples would plunge beneath the waterfall.

I never saw anyone stay under the bone-numbing cascade as long as one particular woman. I'd seen her practicing on several occasions and met her once while hiking down the mountain one evening. She told me she was of Korean descent and a follower of Korean Zen. I asked her about her training, and without much prompting, she explained very frankly how the discipline of the waterfall practice had cured her of acute depression that had crippled her for years. I'd asked her how she thought the waterfall training had helped. She said that it took great focus of mind to master this feat—there was just no room left for depression. Under the waterfall she looked supernatural and serene, as if oblivious to the ice-cold flow. She radiated vitality.

Because of the shakuhachi, visitors saw me as something of an enigma. Hearing the sound of the flute from a distance well before they saw me, they were given no advance warning about the flute-playing "Martian" who was standing around the corner. When they did finally see me, they were usually stunned into silence. I could see them searching the content of their mental filing systems, and then, after a couple of seconds of processing without finding any matching image, there'd be a complete expiration of air which always seemed to carry the sound "Ehhhhhhhh!"

Because of my "Martian" status, I was continuously photographed alongside husbands, wives, mothers with children, and groups of all types. One keen photographer introduced himself as Kabota, president of Shinjuku Ward Camera Club. He handed me his name card.

"You come here next Sunday?" he asked.

"Yes," I answered, not knowing his reason for asking.

"Goodo. All camera club come take the picture you," he said.

"Wonderful," I said. *Dreadful!* I thought.

Apparently, Sunday was the camera club's monthly outing, and they had chosen Mount Takeo as their location. True to his word, Kabota-san arrived on Sunday, a most brilliant day, followed by at least twenty-five enthusiastic camera buffs sporting Nikons, Hasselblads, Canons, and Leicas. Huffing and sweating, they carried tripods and huge telephoto lenses that could likely take pictures of Mars. Their dress reflected their seriousness and distinguished them from the common specimen of "the sightseer." Each person wore a photographer's sleeveless vest, the pockets bulging, no doubt with endless rolls of film.

Kabota spotted me and gave a shout of recognition, then proudly directed the group, which looked to him as a finder of great treasure. After a long speech about the subject—me—the group excitedly scampered into position several feet from where I stood. Then Kabota gave the order to shoot!

Dozens of flashes exploded like fireworks, taking me a little by surprise. The flute fell away from my mouth, but, quickly chastised, I carried on with my playing. Passersby too polite or frightened to walk through the photo zone were forced to wait on either side of the action. Everywhere I looked, a camera looked back at me. Even nonmembers pointed their cameras and joined in the frenzy! Kabota called a halt, and calm settled again on the mountain path. Some of those people who where holding back made a dash while it was safe.

Kabota walked up to me, and I drew breath to exchange a few pleasantries, pleased that I could maintain my Japanese-style courtesy in this most awkward circumstance. My intention was cut short as Kabota wordlessly reached out and clutched my chin, twisting it north, for another perspective. He rushed back into position. More pedestrians made a break for it, crouching with their heads down, a hand raised in surrender. Someone fired before Kabota's signal, and he turned to glare at the offender for a few seconds, displaying the full extent of his displeasure. He let off a volley of clicks, and hundreds more echoed. I thought maybe they would run out of ammo, but they just reloaded again and again. Then Kabota lowered his camera, signaling, I thought, the end of the shoot. I was horribly wrong. Each and every one of them wanted a personal photograph with me!

I stood there while they swapped cameras and had a photo taken with me. Hand on shoulder, shaking hands, holding the flute, playing the flute. *Next please! This was real spiritual training,* I thought. Kabota was the last, and when he came up he grabbed my hand and smiled into the cameras and they all took pictures of "Kabota the president." By the last ten or so pictures, I had ceased smiling.

Kabota then let go of my hand, but the torture continued. With Kabota leading the way, I was given a standing ovation by both club members and the stranded crowds. Then, Kabota began to make a speech, giving details of their next photo opportunity, which apparently was at the summit in thirty minutes.

Everyone fell in behind Kabota, and with a chorus of *"Say-ohnara, sayohnara,"* they were all off. Within a few meters Kabota halted, causing a nasty pileup. He turned and walked back to me and asked, awkwardly, "Please, you give your living place." I wrote my address on a piece of paper and gave it to him. He shook my hand, bowed, then waved his arm towards the summit and was off.

Three weeks later I received a large envelope in the mail. Inside were at least fifty photographs, almost all identical but with slight angle changes. Some photos had personal notes and cards attached. I could identify the photographs taken first and those taken near the end of the session by the fading smile on my face. One card read: *"Ray-san, we enjoy very much the day. You think I great player, thank you. Signed Kabota Kenji."*

The main temple of Mount Takeo is named Yakuoin Yukiji. It is the sacred temple of Mount Takeo and enshrines the Buddha, Lord of Medicine. Temples in Japan frequently represent something secular. For example, you can visit a temple to pray to the Buddha of traffic safety. Another temple may help in family matters or in finding a husband. There's even a temple were people go to ask for help in passing exams.

For centuries Yakuoin Yukiji has been a center, like so many mountain temples in Japan, for shugendo, the ascetic path to realization. Some of the followers of shugendo, who still exist today, call themselves *yama-bushi,* or mountain dwellers. They solemnly place their faith in the mystical powers of the mountain. By chance, I met one of these mountain dwellers late in November, towards the end of my shugyo.

In the quietness of the early morning, my breath flowed through the bamboo, carrying the notes, which then drifted into nothingness. I stood on the side of this sacred mountain, feeling the security of the large cedar tree behind me. Ten minutes earlier I had hidden behind it to change into a fresh shirt, the old one sweat-soaked from the arduous climb. It felt exhilarating playing in the cold, golden morning light. My head was clear, and my body tingled from the long trek.

I immersed myself in my playing. The day was perfectly still, and I felt as if I was the only person on the mountain. Hearing the tinkling of a bell, I looked up. Coming towards me in the distance was an extraordinary sight: a monk striding down from the summit, clad in white and framed by a rhapsody of fall colors. He looked like a huge, white-winged Japanese crane. As he came closer, I ceased playing. Interrupting the silence was the sound of his low, sonorous mutterings, which I assumed were Buddhist sutras. He walked within speaking distance and came to a halt. His eyes bore into me longer than was comfortable. Then with a slight nod he said, "Dozo," instructing me to play.

Without comment, I obediently placed the flute to my lips and blew a meditative sutra melody. As I played, we stared at each other. He was elderly and looked like he'd stepped out of another century. On his head he wore an elongated, boat-shaped straw hat. He was dressed in a short kimono with winglike sleeves and pants that gathered below the knee, with twine running from calf to ankle. His forearms were covered with the same cloth as his pants, and he carried a bag over his left shoulder. On his feet he wore roughly made straw sandals.

He listened carefully and silently until I finished.

"Domo arigato gozaimasu," he thanked me with a slight bow, and then said, "Shakuhachi muzukashi desu ne. Very difficult, isn't it?"

"Hai," I responded in agreement and then asked him, "Have you traveled far today, Sensei?"

"About twenty kilometers from the other side of the summit." He pointed back towards the direction from which he had come.

"You must have started early this morning."

"Sunrise," he said. "Your sound carries far," he said, pointing at the flute. "I heard you from quite a distance." He told me that it had been pleasant catching the melody of the shakuhachi on the breeze. At first he had thought it was coming from the temples below.

"I am very surprised to see a foreigner up here playing shakuhachi."

"Yes, it must seem quite strange." I replied.

"Where did you learn shakuhachi? You play very traditionally." His words seemed to come from the depths of his abdomen.

"I study with a master in Tokyo, Sensei."

"Shakuhachi is not so popular now. Years ago in Kyoto I would see monks on the streets playing. I don't see any now," he said.

"Is your temple in Kyoto, Sensei?" I asked.

"Yes, on Mount Hiei. I'm Gyoja monk."

I was amazed and looked at him in bewilderment. Here before me was a "running Buddha" of sacred Mount Hiei. I had heard of their incredible marathon runs. These mountain ascetics were initiated into Buddhahood by running marathon distances daily for a period of one hundred consecutive days. In persevering through the harshest of privations, it was said that they were reborn with the completion of their marathon run.

"*Hajime mashite,* Sensei. Pleased to meet you," I said, bowing respectfully.

A guttural acknowledgment escaped from his mouth. "Hajime mashite dozo *yoroshiku onegaishimasu.*"

I sensed he might leave, so I quickly blurted out, "Have you completed the one hundred–day marathon, Sensei?"

"Ah, you know *kaihogyo,*" he replied, nodding and saying, "Hai."

In Japanese and broken English, he told his story. When language was insufficient, he used hand gestures. At sometime in his life this elderly monk had run twenty-six miles each day for one hundred consecutive days, praying at over two hundred sacred temples and shrines. On one of those days he had to run thirty-one miles, entering the city of Kyoto to pray at the main temples. Each day of running took around seven hours.

He told me how his legs and feet had throbbed and become infected through cuts and sores, and how he had suffered from diarrhea in the first forty days. I was surprised when he said that

179

the worst was over by day sixty. By then the sores had healed into calluses, and his sickness had passed. With his hands on his stomach, he talked of the need for great spiritual strength, not physical strength, he explained, squeezing the muscle of his upper arm. He went on to tell me of the cord and knife he carried to remind him of his duty to take his life either by hanging or disemboweling himself if he failed to finish the one hundred days.

"Strong spirit must have for reach end," he said. I listened intently, occasionally looking away for a brief respite from his piercing black eyes—eyes that made me question my own seriousness.

Deciding it was time to stop talking, he gazed even deeper into my eyes and unexpectedly asked why I had chosen this particular place to play. I explained the need for my daily hike and for a quiet place to play shakuhachi. I also explained my sixty-day shugyo, feeling fraudulent in the face of the rigorous disciplines he had just described.

"It's good that you have a discipline. The mind gets disorderly and wears itself out without it. Discipline holds the spirit and body together," he said, pausing to look in the direction he was heading.

"Where are you going today, Sensei?" I asked feeling a little disappointed that he might leave.

"Yakuoin Yukiji, the sacred temple of Takeo," he answered.

"Would you like to share food with me?" I asked diffidently, my motive a little selfish. I wanted to hear more from him. He smiled and pointed to an open area with a view of the hills. We walked to it, and he sat down and asked me to join him. He opened his bag and removed his own food. I did the same. We sat quietly, sharing our food and water. He ate only a small portion.

"Too much food no good," he said patting his stomach, then his head.

"Have you done the long Gyoja fast, Sensei?" He slowly reflected, then responded, "Hai."

"Would you mind telling me about it?" I asked.

He thought for a while, then began painstakingly explaining his eight-day fast.

For several weeks before the fast he had reduced his intake of food and water. He said the first day was no problem. By the second and third he had experienced some nausea. On the fourth day the nausea and hunger had gone away. By the end of the fifth day, he said he could taste blood, and began to dehydrate. At this point in his explanation, he paused and stressed a lack of water by sucking in his checks and shrinking his body. Because there was no saliva, he had accepted an offer from his attendant monk to rinse his mouth with water, on the condition that he spit it all back into a cup. By the seventh day he was on the brink of death.

"No food difficult. No water difficult. Sitting Buddha-way most difficult!" he exclaimed.

I took Buddha-way to mean zazen. I thought of the excruciating pain I had experienced while sitting in zazen for only short periods of time. He allowed himself twenty minutes walking a day, but on the sixth and seventh days he was unable to walk for this long.

"Seven day, all gone," he said, and made a gesture with his hand to indicate that something had left his head. Then he cupped his ear. "Hear everything big." He pointed to his nose. "Smell everything big."

We sat surrounded by stillness until a whispering flurry of leaves came and seemed to remind him it was time to move on. He rose to his feet.

"*Omanek domo arigato.* Thank you for inviting me," he said with a bow.

"Domo arigato, Sensei," I responded simply.

I followed him back to the path. He placed his hand on his abdomen and said, "Buddha mind not thinking, Buddha mind like thunder."

After a brief moment he said, "Dozo, please," and gestured for me to play my shakuhachi. He then bowed, turned, and walked off.

I experienced a new vigor on the days that immediately followed my encounter with the marathon monk of Mount Hiei. My shugyo had a much-needed boost, and each hike up Mount Takeo gained new momentum.

With the weather becoming much colder, the final days of my shugyo were incredibly difficult, but there were states of clarity where "emptiness" had a different meaning from the emptiness I had once known. This emptiness wasn't dominated by fear or desire. There was a sense of "completeness" that allowed me to be detached from my thoughts, yet when needed, I could reflect objectively and without distortion.

By the end of sixty days I had completed around three hundred hours of flute playing and had hiked almost four hundred miles up and down the mountain.

I walked down to the Yakuoin Yukiji Temple, feeling a curious mix of relief and sadness. I was glad that it was over, but I also felt as if I'd lost something deeply personally.

As I sat in the hall, waiting to tell the monks I had completed my shugyo, I smiled at how much I'd become attached to the last sixty days. The smile on my face soon turned into giggles, and then uncontrollable laughter the more I thought about it. I was still laughing as the monks arrived. They probably thought I'd gone mad. By the time they reached me, they had joined in, actually laughing even harder than I was.

杉
凤
之 <u>Chapter Fifteen</u>
調 Breath of the Ancients

Even though strenuous days on Mount Takeo had left me exhausted, I continued attending shakuhachi classes. Yokoyama, unaware of my shugyo, commented weekly on my extraordinary progress, encouraging me onward. During these lessons my tiredness was almost an advantage, removing any self-consciousness and allowing me to play the music without the interference of thought.

Since I'd started with Yokoyama, I'd memorized and moved through several honkyuko pieces, and, because of my intense practice on the mountain, felt I had added another layer to each of them. I could now play my most recently assigned piece, "Sagariha," or "Falling Leaves," from memory, and hoped Yokoyama would give me my next piece after tonight's lesson.

That evening during a break, one of the newer students brought up the topic of a rebel shakuhachi player who had recently performed at the famous Blue Note jazz club in New York City. His name was Akikazu Nakamura, and he was apparently a former student of Yokoyama. Some of the students knew him well and told me that he had started his own school in Roka Koen, a small community in the western suburbs of Tokyo.

One of the students said he had been to see Nakamura in concert recently and had enjoyed a couple of the jazz numbers he'd played. He then enthusiastically mentioned that Nakamura had also performed a well-known honkyoku piece called "San-an." During one of the long, complicated parts of this piece, Nakamura hadn't taken a single breath, he said. Nobody seemed particularly surprised or interested except for the student telling the story and myself. It was evidently common knowledge that Nakamura had developed this rather unusual breathing technique and often at his concerts introduced it to the audience as "circular breathing." Yokoyama's only comment was: "There is no need for circular breathing when playing honkyoku." I could see what he meant, as each phrase of the music had been perfectly written to be played with one complete breath. Nevertheless, I wanted to find out more about it.

The conversation quickly and protectively turned into a discussion about whether the shakuhachi with all its tradition should be playing jazz or other types of avant-garde and contemporary music. A few students, unable to make the leap into any kind of change, resisted the notion, but most seemed to agree that any music, if played well, could only be good for the future of shakuhachi.

Throughout the discussion my thoughts stayed with this rebel player Nakamura and his circular breathing. The technique wasn't new to me. It was something I had already tried on the shakuhachi, but with little success. How had Nakamura managed to do it?

It was almost time for Yokoyama's break to end. There were two students before me. I sat waiting and thinking about my introduction to circular breathing the previous year in India.

Dianne and I were taking a much-needed three-month break from Japan just before I started studying with Yokoyama. We'd returned to our favorite spot, Dharamsala in northern India. Dharamsala, or, to be more accurate, McLeod Ganj, is home to the exiled Tibetan government, the Dalai Lama, and hundreds of circular-breathing monks.

During previous visits to Dharamsala, in my pre-flute days, I'd paid little attention to the breathing phenomenon that surrounded me, but with my recent interest in the shakuhachi I was now curious about any and all breathing techniques. In the past, Dianne and I had just sat quietly within the grounds of Nymgyl Monastery, simply listening to the continuous drone of the long Tibetan horns and enjoying the atmosphere. But on our most recent visit, I could be seen standing only inches away from a horn-blowing monk, scrutinizing his every breath. Clad in a voluminous burgundy robe and wearing imitation Nike runners and bright red socks, the young celibate stood with eyes half-shut in meditation, playing a nine-foot long horn.

As usual, our lingering presence had attracted a few monks who wanted to see what I was up to. They moved in unselfconsciously for a closer look. Puzzled, I kept repeating, "It's impossible, it's impossible," to Dianne, who was standing behind me. Tenzing, a monk we'd known for several years, saw us and walked over. In his delightfully accented English, he asked me what was so impossible. I explained that I was baffled about how the monk was blowing the continuous note without taking a breath. Smiling as he adjusted his Dalai Lama-style glasses, he said, "I am afraid it is nothing mystical. It is a very simple technique. We can all do it with practice."

He went on to explain how they would blow out through their mouths and breathe in through their noses at the same time. "We must keep our cheeks full with the pressure of air. Watch me." He began sniffing and blowing, sniffing and blowing. I was no wiser. The player I'd been watching earlier stopped blowing, and Tenzing took the horn and swung it towards himself. He started blowing as you would with a trumpet, sniffing and blowing. His cheeks remained full the entire time.

"Here, please. You try it," he said, handing me the horn. I hesitated, seeing how wet it was with saliva. Untucking my T-shirt, I roughly wiped the spittle away, then placed it reluctantly to my lips.

Getting a sound out of the horn was not that difficult, though my effort certainly lacked volume. Putting the breathing theory into practice was extremely challenging. I could sniff, then blow, but I couldn't sniff and blow at the same time. The monks watching were all laughing and trying to give me advice in a mixture of Hindi, Tibetan, and English. Desperate to spit, I handed back the instrument and, grinning, said again, "It's impossible!"

Tenzing enthusiastically said, "We need water and small pipe. Then I can teach you very, very quickly."

"Pipe?" I asked, confused.

"Yes, for drinking."

"Ah! A straw," I said.

The monks looked on the ground for a discarded straw. One walked over to a pile of dirty dishes that sat next to an outside tap. Dianne, seeing the horror in my eyes, quickly took a pen from her pouch, dismantled it with her knife, and handed me the hollow tube along with her water bottle.

"Swiss Army wife to the rescue!" she exclaimed.

Tenzing filled his mouth with water. Then, as he inhaled through his nose, he simultaneously squirted the water out from his mouth in a long thin jet, propelling it about four feet in front of him and scattering three or four monks. My turn. I'd spat water out like this thousands of times as a kid, but never sniffing in air at the same time. I tried a couple of dry runs, then filled my mouth with water. I was concentrating so hard on sniffing that the water just literally fell from my mouth. After several more attempts and a lot of laughing, my chin, T-shirt, trousers, and feet were soaked. The monks seemed to think this was the greatest thing and were laughing so hard they had to hang on to one another.

Soon I got the hang of it, and Tenzing took me to the next level. Filling one of the dirty dishes with water from Dianne's bottle and using the substitute straw, he began demonstrating skillfully, by blowing a continuous stream of bubbles—sniffing and blowing, sniffing and blowing. Handing me back my pen tube, he then directed me to do the same. Blowing too hard, the water overflowed from the bowl, soaking me yet again.

"If you practice this every day, you will soon be able to do it," Tenzing said.

He was right. I persisted, and within a few days, I could blow and sniff at the same time. I could keep the bubbles moving indefinitely.

After I got the hang of it, they let me practice on a short horn. Soon I was allowed to join them on the long horn.

Through Tenzing, I had become close enough with the horn players to ask them if it would be possible to play the shakuhachi while they played the Tibetan long horn. They agreed and suggested that some of the other monks at their monastery might like to perform some tonal chanting. I wondered if the two instruments and the chanting would blend, and hoped that the long horn wouldn't drown out the shakuhachi.

We set a date for the following Tuesday.

On the night of the performance, there were ten chanters, four long horn players and about twenty onlookers waiting for me in the monastery. I was greeted by Tenzing and led into the main hall. The electricity lines had been down in this area for the last two days, so the monks had filled the room with oil lamps and a mixture of wax and butter candles. I'd never seen the monastery lit up at night and found the glow, along with the smell of incense, wood smoke, and bodies, delightful.

The soot-blackened wooden beams running across the roof were evidence of many a power failure over the years. Colorful silk scroll paintings hung from each wall and were softly illuminated. Several pictures of the Dalai Lama smiled down at us. The huge golden Buddha at the back of the hall, surrounded by flowers, brass pots, jugs, bowls and an assortment of bells, reflected every single flame in the room.

We all agreed our recital should be without a break. The monks would chant alone for a while. Then the horns would start and hold a continuous, steady, low drone. I would come in when I thought the time was right.

What followed was extraordinary. The deep guttural chanting created a primitive yet meaningful sense of being. When the horns started up they seemed to move the air. The sound was hypnotic. It was an effort to introduce the flute; I just wanted to stand there and listen. The first union was only marginally consonant, the overtones bordering on chaos. Then I found the pitch that brought it all together. I played a combination of only six notes in the upper octave, blowing long tones with a few adjoining riffs. The rich tones of the horns and the chanting reverberated like souls in exile, the flute the liberator, flushing the body with emotion.

"Ray-san!" At the sound of Yokoyama's voice, I was quickly brought back to Japan.

"Hi!" I shouted, as I leapt to my feet. No matter how accustomed I became to playing in front of Yokoyama, when he called me for my lesson, my stomach always jumped. I confidently walked up to the table, placing my music sheet face down. This gesture indicated that I had memorized my assigned music well enough that I wished to be tested.

After the usual formalities, I asked Yokoyama if I could stand because it was difficult for me to perform "Sagariha" in the seated position. To play the piece I had to use an extremely taxing breathing technique called *komibuki*. Komibuki creates a kind of unrefined vibrato effect. To achieve it, one must first fully inhale, allowing the abdomen to fill and expand outwardly like a balloon. The air is then slowly released through the shakuhachi in a controlled succession of quick, short bursts from the diaphragm. Performed properly, it can take a player into deeper levels of concentration and meditation. It also warms the body very quickly, so I often relied on the technique during cold mornings on Mount Takeo. Sasaki had told me how komuso monks had used this method themselves while sitting in the snow. He said the heat generated from their bodies melted a circle around them.

By the expression on Yokoyama's face as the last note faded into silence, I could tell I had played it well. He said that I must have studied hard and that it was a good effort. Then he asked me to play it again. This time he would play along with me. Rather than concentrating on my own playing, I merely went through the motions so that I could listen and watch him intently. Yokoyama's brilliance reminded me just how far one could take this instrument. And how far I had to go.

Yokoyama would never actually say you'd passed. He'd simply recommend a new piece if he was satisfied.

After we bowed, he said, "Next week please practice 'San-an.'"

Yes! I thought. I bowed and thanked him.

"San-an" was the composition that I most wanted to learn. It was a long and very powerful piece. It was considered very demanding and highly complex, and covered the entire range of techniques. Traditionally, it had been played as a prayer to assist in the safe and easy delivery of babies. Before a woman went into labor, the komuso monk would ceremoniously pour grains of rice through the barrel of the shakuhachi. While the rice was cooking, he would play "San-an," then give the cooked rice to the woman.

Savoring my fleeting moment of glory, I decided to stay a while and listen to the master. My appreciation of honkyoku was developing. I now had a clearer understanding and aesthetic sense of the finer points of the music. The pieces were like Zen koans, to be worked on, grasped, then let go.

Yokoyama called up his next student, an older man who was having some difficulty adjusting to the new flute he'd bought from sensei the week before. The student said it was sitting too high on his chin. Yokoyama took the flute, examined it, blew it, and then got up and walked over to his tool box. He pulled out a huge file, looked at it, changed his mind, and swapped it for a smaller one. I watched in amazement, looking from Yokoyama to the student and back, as Yokoyama began to vigorously rasp away at the mouthpiece of this six thousand dollar flute. Nobody blinked. When he was done, the student took it and placed it back on his chin, wiggled it into position, blew a note, and said, "Thank you very much, Sensei."

On the way home that night, Kazu told me that it wasn't uncommon to work on "San-an" for up to three years before Yokoyama let you move on. Thinking of what I'd heard of

Nakamura's circular-breathing approach to "San-an," I asked Kazu if he had ever seen Nakamura perform.

"Yes, once. I like his honkyoku very much, but the contemporary music he sometimes plays is not interesting for me," he said. "Why don't you go and see him, Ray? I think he's holding a concert at NHK Hall sometime next month."

Anxious to see this shakuhachi rebel in a live performance, I asked Dianne if she would like to go with me.

We arrived at the concert hall early and found seats in the front row, dead center. I wanted to be sure to see everything. I noticed in the program that Nakamura would play "San-an."

At 7:00 PM the concert hall darkened, and a small, barely visible figure gracefully glided to center stage. A single spotlight came on, shining only on the flute. Nakamura paused for about thirty seconds, then began to play.

I heard something of Yokoyama's influence in his music, but noticed that he had developed a sound of his own. His music contained the remarkable timbre and tone color that had originally brought me to this instrument. He had a strikingly different blowing technique and played with tremendous energy. After he finished playing the piece called "Koku," or "Empty Sky," the appreciative audience's applause quickly dispersed the highly charged atmosphere. My curiosity had been rewarded. He was great.

The next piece was a duet called "Shika no Tone," or "Distant Cry of the Deer," and another shakuhachi player came on stage and joined Nakamura.

After playing a couple of less memorable contemporary pieces, Nakamura announced that the last solo of the evening would be "San-an."

From a number of flutes, Nakamura picked up the longest, which was about thirty-five inches in length. Then once again he paused, allowing the audience to quiet down.

I listened and watched intently. Nakamura played brilliantly, and his impeccable sense of timing filled the music with numerous meaningful silences. That silence is called *ma* in Japanese music and doesn't only refer to music. It refers to the silence between all sounds, and is especially poignant in nature. Ma is that fathomless space between the hoots of an owl or the irregular chirps of crickets. It's the stillness after the cicada stops.

Halfway through the piece, Nakamura began to perform circular breathing. For over three minutes, there wasn't a break in the sound. The effect was dynamic. He had taken "San-an" beyond music and into something bordering on the mystical.

After cultural concerts in Japan, it's usually customary for the performers to go to the foyer and thank the guests for attending. Dianne and I waited patiently, and after about ten minutes Nakamura appeared. Several people gathered and began bowing and congratulating him. More were waiting.

When Nakamura was free, I approached, and, like the others, congratulated him on his awesome performance. He modestly thanked me. Not having the required level of Japanese language skills or the time to do the etiquette dance around the issue, I got quickly to the point by telling him I was studying shakuhachi. Before I could continue with my rehearsed speech, he said, in good clear English, "Oh really! What style have you chosen to study?"

There are few Japanese shakuhachi masters in the world, and fewer still who can communicate so well in English. I had finally found one who might be able to teach me some of the subtleties of shakuhachi by using the English language.

I told him I was studying honkyoku.

"Ah yes. A very good choice. Who is your teacher?"

"Katsuya Yokoyama," I said.

"Yokoyama Katsuya," he replied. "He is my teacher too. I studied with him for many years."

We talked a little about Yokoyama, and then I got straight to the point and asked if it would be possible to take lessons from him while still studying with Yokoyama. As tactfully as possible, I explained that I definitely didn't want to give up Yokoyoma's class. He agreed that I shouldn't and said that there was no one better to study under. I said I was worried about the possible conflict that might be caused between the two teachers. He nodded and thought for a moment, then said, "For Japanese this would be a little difficult, but it's possible. I would be happy to teach you. After all, we are all part of the same Yokoyama-Watazumi-do lineage. But if you do decide to study with me, perhaps you should first discuss it with Sensei."

As a foreigner, I knew I had a sort of diplomatic immunity when it came to the complexities of Japanese etiquette and protocol. I was not expected to know the rules, so I could break them without too much offense. If a foreigner was sensitive with the Japanese, there was never a problem.

"Yes, I'll do that," I replied.

After a few more questions, I asked Nakamura if he had taught circular breathing to any of his students. He would teach them, he said, but none had yet reached the required level. I mentioned that I had learned how to circular breathe in India on a Tibetan horn but had not been able to do it on the shakuhachi. He explained that this method could only be used on instruments such as trumpets and horns but could not be applied to shakuhachi. His method was completely different.

"It's difficult to blow a flute when your cheeks are puffed like a bullfrog. You have to learn how to manipulate the throat area," he said.

Realizing I was taking up too much of his time, I apologized and asked if I could call him within the next few days. He handed me his name card and said I should telephone his secretary and make an appointment. Shaking hands, we said good-bye.

I met with Yokoyama the next day, and explained that because of my limited time in Japan, I felt I should be taking more lessons. This came as no surprise to him, as I had previously asked if it would be possible to study with him more often than I already did. He had told me, at that time, that it was difficult, as he wasn't always in Tokyo. When Yokoyama wasn't teaching, lecturing, or performing in concerts, he was constantly traveling between his studio in Okayama and his studio in Tokyo, which are about four hundred and fifty kilometers apart. Not wanting to offend Yokoyama in any way, I tactfully suggested the possibility of studying with another teacher as well as himself. He immediately asked which teacher I had in mind. When I told him Nakamura Sensei, he said exactly what I had expected him to say: Nakamura was a fine and adventurous young player and his lessons would be of great value to me.

Within a week, I was sitting in front of Nakamura for my first lesson. Foregoing the usual formalities and time-consuming etiquette, he thankfully got straight down to business. Having never heard me play before, he told me to warm up for a few moments and then, when I was ready, to play "Honshirabe" for him. This piece would give him a good sampling of my ability and technique.

"Good. You play well. You must have worked very hard," he said. "Okay now, Ray. There are two things I want to show you. The first is a completely new way of breathing, a more efficient way that will give you much more control over the air flow."

He repositioned the angle of my head and adjusted the embouchure, then asked me to blow "more down" into the flute. With my chin closer to my chest and my lower lip farther inside the flute, I tried to play. It felt peculiar and awkward.

We practiced this for a while, and each time I lost the position Nakamura patiently readjusted and corrected me.

"The second change I want you to make is the way you move your head. Instead of moving it up and down, I want you to try moving it at a slight angle from side to side. It will feel like starting over again for a short time. Within a couple of weeks you'll know what I'm talking about," he said. "Practice, Ray, and when you can do it comfortably, call me. Then we will arrange your next lesson."

Nakamura worked with me on these techniques and very little else for almost six months.

Having the input and expertise of two teachers was benefiting me greatly, and if Yokoyama ever noticed any of the subtle changes that were taking place, he never mentioned it to me.

Breath was always the most important topic with Nakamura. He taught me how to economize my exhalations so that I could play longer notes, and he showed me exercises to develop my diaphragm. Each new technique came with an explanation and a question period. He constantly corrected my posture and fingering techniques. I felt extremely fortunate to have met him.

Almost a year to the day from my first lesson, he announced that he would show me his method of circular breathing. He explained that he would show me as much as possible but that some of it was difficult to put into words, so I would have to work it out for myself.

Circular breathing had taken Nakamura four years to develop. He hadn't had a teacher, so he had worked it out entirely for himself. I was grateful that he was willing to share this hard-earned technique with me.

Standing over the sink in the kitchen, Nakamura asked me to demonstrate the continuous-bubble trick with a straw and water. This I did without any spillage on the kitchen floor. Then we went back into his studio, where Nakamura handed me a child's small yellow, red, and blue plastic trumpet. Nakamura sat opposite me with a trumpet just as colorful.

He puffed out his cheeks like Dizzy Gillespie and began wailing out a steady, continuous note. He wasn't stopping, so I joined him. My training with the Tibetans was now really paying off. As long as I kept a steady pressure in my cheeks, I could simultaneously inhale through my nose and exhale into the trumpet. The sound was unbearable, and I'm sure the sight was ridiculous. Nakamura explained again that this method was all right for musical instruments where you could maintain a pressure with the cheeks, but it was ineffectual for shakuhachi. At least it had one thing in common with his method: You inhaled through your nose as you blew out through your mouth at the same time.

Laughing at the noise we'd created between us, he said that the easy part was over and that he would demonstrate the technique without bellowing the cheeks. As I watched, I noticed a slight movement in his Adam's apple area. He told me to concentrate on the throat and imagine swallowing air, and at the same time try to visualize opening and closing my throat like a valve.

His only response to my barrage of questions was "I can't explain it to you exactly, Ray, but just remember that if I can do it, then so can you."

I kept trying, but without the pressure in the cheeks, there was always a gap between exhaling and inhaling. Nakamura kept repeating, "You must try to visualize yourself opening and closing your throat like a valve. I can do it, so you can do it!"

He was right; I could, but it took me two years.

Chapter Sixteen
R.S.V.P. or Else!

For the past two weeks we had suffered heavy rain that left Tokyo streaked with all the accumulated grime and pollution of the winter. It had become a monochromatic city. Most of my time was spent in the recesses of the earth, moving from one interior to the next, either through subways, underground walkways, or underground shopping centers.

As the downpours persisted, everything started to look a little fresher between cloudbursts. The most noticeable difference was in the greenery. With the thick coating of dust washed away, the shrubs and trees and little patches of grass started to breathe again. Their shades of green took on new brightness, and their growth seemed less restricted. As the skies finally began to break up, the days grew warmer and clearer. It was safe to walk the streets again—the deadly eye-level umbrellas had vanished.

After spending so many days avoiding the rain, it felt great to flee the confinement of the city and hike the misty trails of Mount Takeo once more.

It had been over three months since I had visited the mountain. The last time was on the final day of my shugyo. It was a Saturday, and, with the weather change, there would be more people on the trails. I had decided to avoid taking the main route up and instead hiked on to a steep, unmarked trail. Following a small but swollen stream, I clambered over slippery boulders and fallen trees. The noise of the flowing water filled my ears, and the ground had a damp, earthy smell. Changing direction slightly, and with the sounds of the stream now far behind, I stopped, sat on a rock, and savored the quietness. It felt good to be alone.

The luxury of silence ended after about thirty minutes when I heard a group of hikers way off in the distance. I left the rock and walked farther into the woods to avoid having to greet them. It wasn't unusual for a well-spaced line of hikers to pass and for each one of them to greet you exuberantly. From the time I'd heard them coming until they were well past me and out of sight, there was never a break in their conversation. I waited until their voices faded then continued my walk.

Thirsty from the hike, I entered the little teashop below the temple and was greeted with "Irasshaimase. Welcome." Then quickly a voice said, "Ah, Ray-san, long time no see. Please come in."

Dianne and I had known the owner and his wife for some time now and always enjoyed stopping by for a chat before we went hiking or before my practice. The place was empty. The group of hikers that had passed me hadn't stopped. They were trying to reach the summit before lunch.

The teashop owner, Iijima-san, was sitting at one of the tables with a completely dismantled toaster oven in front of him. There were bits everywhere. We both laughed at the sight, and I asked him what was wrong with it. At his invitation I sat down, and soon his wife brought us both large cups of tea and some rice balls.

"He has no idea what he's doing, Ray-san. He's been tinkering with that all morning," she said affectionately, talking about her husband in the third person.

Together, we examined all the parts, and soon I saw the problem; the points on the thermostat's switch were blackened with carbon.

"Easily fixed," I said, as I began filing away the buildup.

As he put the thing back together, I munched on a rice ball, feeling pleased that I could help. We started talking about all the latest scandals in the news, and Iijima-san grumbled on about the terrible corruption and dishonesty in the higher ranks of society. His wife came out from the kitchen and fondly scolded him again.

"Is he talking about depressing things, Ray-san?" She then deftly changed the subject, asking me if I had seen the recent pictures in the paper of Masako, the young woman who was dating Prince Hironomiya. "Isn't she pretty, ne! Doesn't she dress beautifully, ne! She's studied abroad, you know."

One or two people came into the shop, and soon the owner's young daughter was dashing around serving teas and little snacks. Then four men, laughing and joking, came through the door, making a great deal of noise. They were instantly recognizable as yakuza, or Japanese gangsters. Iijima's wife quickly showed them to a large table and rushed off to get tea while they looked at the menu.

They were a fascinating sight, and I couldn't help but stare at them at every possible chance. They were like caricatures from a hammy gangster movie. Their clothes and their every gesture seemed so contrived, so utterly exaggerated and comical. I'd always thought that Japanese actors overacted when playing the part of yakuza. Not so; they were right on.

One of the men, obviously higher ranked than the others, was wearing the mandatory baggy black suit with a dark purple shirt, yellow tie, and black patent leather shoes. Around his neck he wore what looked like an Olympic gold medal on a thick chain, and each time he leaned forward it hit the table with a clunk. *He probably received it for "Most Suffering Caused" player of the year,* I thought. On his right wrist was a heavy gold bracelet, and on his fingers were several large rings.

His peons, equally conspicuous, had tightly permed hair, dark glasses, and the uniform of the lower ranks. One was sporting a bomber jacket and black shiny track pants. His face left you with no lingering doubt of his sincere devotion to violence. Another was in a yellowish sports jacket, golfing pants, a knit shirt, and white patent leather slip-on shoes with a gold bar across the front. *You look like a right tosser!* I shouted, in my mind.

The third peon, perhaps slightly higher ranked, was wearing a black calf-length, Gestapo-style leather coat, black pants, and a white polo shirt. You had to be tough to dress like these guys. The thug in the yellow jacket reminded me of a lad I knew in London. He wore a pink suit just so he could attract some "bother." He wasn't up for any criticisms on his fashion choice, as many a poor bastard found out.

The yakuza aren't the romantic, chivalrous chaps portrayed in movies. They run the underworld and are simply racketeers, into gambling, protection, the sex trade, and drugs. Not the sort of people you'd want as pals.

I didn't realize just how long I'd had been staring at them until Iijima-san caught my attention, and with a light touch of my hand and the slightest shake of his head made it known that it was wise not to look at them so obviously.

Iijima's wife took their food order and quickly returned with a tray of sake and beer. I could tell that she wanted Iijima's help, so quietly, I thanked my hosts and said good-bye. As I left Iijima said, "Come back soon, please." Hearing an outburst of raucous laughter coming from the gangsters' table, I shut the door.

As I walked along the path towards my usual spot, I thought about the yakuza story an Israeli fellow called Sol once told me. I'd met him on a train late one evening as I was traveling home from teaching an English class. He was a street vendor who sold small mechanical panda bears just outside Shinjuku Station. I'd seen his stall many times, and I always stopped for a look when I was passing by. His display was really eye-catching. He'd always set the bears up on a large ground sheet, then wind them all up and let them walk around, weaving through fake little bamboo plants. When he was in full swing, there were probably more panda bears on that street corner than in all of northern China.

He told me he made a pretty good living selling these, but he had to pay the local yakuza fifty dollars a day for the privilege of working at that particular spot. For his money, he was given a name card and told to call the number on it at any time if he had problems. They were there to help him!

On the same night that I met him, he agitatedly told me how a noodle seller working his mobile noodle cart had taken his spot. He'd asked the man to move to another area, explaining that he paid the yakuza for this position. The noodle vendor, unimpressed, argued aggressively with Sol and, finally, after some pushing and shoving, the vendor resorted to the "This is my birthright, this is my country" routine. Sol, trying to compromise, told the guy to just move a few meters along; then there would be space enough for both of them.

The vendor ignored that suggestion and started hurling more obscenities. Another aggressive exchange broke out. Sol warned him that he would call his yakuza contact if he didn't move.

Sol was angry as he told me the story and said that he was finally forced to make the call. One lone yakuza member arrived. Parking in a "no parking" zone, he got out of his car, walked over to the cart, and, without one word or glance at the noodle vendor or Sol, tipped the cart over into the street, spilling the dishes, noodles, and cooking equipment onto the road. The gangster then got back into his car and drove off. Problem solved. There was no discrimination with these men. It was simply business. If you paid your insurance money, you got your protection, whoever you were. Ugly world. I wondered what a second visit would entail.

I began playing at my usual site around 11:30 AM. Within ten minutes a group of young teenagers came by, escorted by an adult. They were all dressed in identical baseball outfits from caps to shoes. *Baseball shugyo,* I thought.

As they neared, I started to play a few bars of "Kimigayo," the Japanese national anthem. The adult stopped the group with a raise of his hand and instantly removed his hat; the teenagers automatically followed suit. I didn't have the heart to stop halfway, so I completed the anthem. The group chuckled amongst themselves, replaced their hats, bowed, and thanked me, then set off for the summit to picnic, throw balls at one another, and hopefully catch a glimpse of Mount Fuji.

At noon the main temple bell rang, and, as always, I played along with it. If my timing was right, it created an amazing atmosphere, as both my sound and the tolling of the bell blended and echoed across the valley.

With all the dust particles washed from the air, everything around me radiated a brightness. It was a gorgeous day, and everyone who passed stopped for a moment to listen, many commenting on how lovely it was to hear the sound from far off, as they hiked along the path.

Hearing a sudden burst of laughter followed by loud voices, I looked up to see the four characters from the teashop. They were almost upon me. Now worse for sake, and much more boisterous, they stopped and asked me which country I came from. Remaining silent for a moment, I wondered if they'd heard me speaking Japanese this morning in the shop. *Probably not,* I concluded optimistically. Iijima and his wife said good-bye to me in English. So taking a chance, in my worst Japanese, I said I was sorry, but I didn't speak any Japanese. This didn't seem to register with them, and they asked another question. I once again said, "*Wakarimasen*. I don't understand."

"Shakuhachi. You play?" asked the twerp in the yellow jacket.

I was pushing it a bit when I pretended not to understand his English. He demonstrated that he wanted me to play. Touching my flute, he moved it towards my mouth. I blew a simple tune, which seemed to please them. People passing by now didn't stop. The boss, in bits of English, conveyed that I was a good player, and he generously emphasized, "Even Japanese people cannot play shakuhachi not so well!"

His peons, sucking up to their boss, started praising his English ability and then, taking his lead, clapped like idiots. Tossing some money down on to my music sheet, drunkenly, they started to swagger off but suddenly stopped, the peons howling at something the boss had said. Then they all continued towards their temple destination which was only a short distance away.

After about an hour they were back in front of me. This time with extreme politeness, and again trying hard in English, the yellow-jacketed guy whom I now thought of as "Yellow Jacket," indicated that his boss wanted me to come with them to a local restaurant to play shakuhachi.

"No, thank you," I said shaking my head. "I'm sorry."

He asked again, this time even more politely.

"Really. No thank you," I replied, shaking my head again. I distinctly saw him twitch and give the slightest glance towards his boss. He looked uncomfortable and wiped his nose with his thumb and finger. As he did this, I noticed that the top joint of his little finger was missing. I had heard that if a member violated the rules in some way, and if the violation didn't merit expulsion or death, he was forced to cut off the tip of his little finger. The custom was called *yubitsume* in Japanese.

Apparently this custom goes way back to the samurai, when anyone who violated the rules performed yubitsume. This removal of the tip, I'd been told, put them at a great disadvantage when fighting, as it meant they were unable to firmly grip the handle of their sword.

The third time Yellow Jacket asked me to come was unmistakably more than a simple request. I could tell he was under pressure not to make any mistakes in front of his boss. I shuddered to think what would have happened if I refused again. There would be no way for him to back down without losing face in front of his superior. At the very least, my shakuhachi would surely be tossed back from whence it came.

When I agreed to come, he physically let out the breath he'd been holding. He relaxed.

What could they do to me? I thought as we traveled down the mountain together in the cable car. They mostly ignored me while they chatted away about foreign women, laughing salaciously at each of their halfwit jokes. They had come in two cars, one a black Mercedes Benz and the other a white Toyota. Both had the obligatory tinted windows. I was asked to travel in the Toyota with the man who had kindly invited me to lunch.

Two minutes into our journey, the inside of the car was filled with cigarette smoke. I was the only one in the back seat, so I opened the electric window next to me, then leaned over and opened the other on the far side of me. The driver, watching all my actions in his rearview mirror, passed on every detail to Yellow Jacket.

Confident that I couldn't understand their Japanese, the driver laughed and said that the hairy barbarian must be hot. His friend thought this was the greatest thing he'd ever heard and went into hysterics. I thought it was pretty funny, too, and wanted to laugh, but didn't, for fear of giving away my advantage. The conversation remained with hairiness and then moved back to foreign women. Thankfully, the restaurant was only about a fifteen-minute drive from Mount Takeo.

In the parking lot were several expensive-looking foreign cars with tinted windows and cell phone aerials. There were several low-ranked yakuza guys hanging around the vehicles—drivers, I guessed. Some, armed with long feather dusters, were cleaning the black exteriors of their cars while others watched on, chatting and smoking. With our driver left behind, I was escorted by Yellow Jacket towards a large building.

Two women in kimonos greeted us at the main entrance and quickly bypassing a busy dining area, led us through a spacious foyer and out into a landscaped garden area. I'd never seen anything like it before. There were probably six or seven thatched cottages which looked like traditional tea ceremony buildings, nestled in amongst bamboo groves and trees. Each cottage was reached by weaving along a freshly washed cobbled path. Next to it was a fast-flowing stream that seemed to be generated artificially. There were several tiny, red arched bridges that had to be negotiated on the journey. The whole area had a pretentious austerity about it, beautifully planned but most definitely artificial.

As we reached the yakuza's reserved cottage, I could hear voices and laughter. Judging by the noise, this was no small luncheon. It sounded more like a bloody convention! Amid smells of sake and cigarette smoke, Yellow Jacket and I removed our shoes.

We entered a large tatami room. I was greeted with some applause and a few cheers. Seated on the floor, along a very well-stocked row of tables, were about fifteen very red-faced, shady-looking men. The invitation must have said, *"Tacky party, dress casually,"* for they were in their finest and flashiest. Giorgio Armani and Ralph Lauren would have groaned if they'd seen the combinations.

The man who had ordered my presence unsteadily got up and walked over to me. In his best English, he thanked me for coming and shook my hand. Everybody clapped and laughed again. Turning dismissively to Yellow Jacket, he instructed him to take care of me. I was seated at the end of the table by the door.

After a guttural and emotional speech directed at two of the men and an official toast, I was told to help myself. With the word "eat," then with the word "drink," the peon with the missing finger pointed towards an assortment of Japanese delicacies. Watching their performance intrigued me. These men seemed to have no private feelings. Every movement was planned and deliberate, and there was definitely an art in their exaggerated actions. I could see the traditional Kabuki theater, the historical television dramas and comedies, in their every move. It was all there. I imagined colorful ink designs under their clothes, large samurai warriors, dragons, and serpents. Yakuza have a penchant for decorating themselves with tattoos that cover most of their bodies.

Yellow Jacket tried his best to communicate with me in Japanese and struggled bravely searching to find the few English words he knew. On each of his frustrating attempts and with a shrug of my shoulders, I said, "Wakarimasen. I don't understand."

Finally he gave up and again pointed at the food. "Eat, drink."

Listening to the men's childish banter reminded me of high school kids who had found a dirty magazine. They had developed their own slang like the Cockneys of London. It was difficult at times to understand what they were talking about but simple to get their gist. They laughed and shouted. They hit and slapped. Yellow Jacket was cracking jokes and was center stage for a few minutes. Then the boss stepped in and decided to tell a story at Yellow Jacket's expense. As his boss started the story, our friend, grinning and protesting weakly, grabbed his groin once or twice.

Apparently Yellow Jacket had gone shopping with a friend for a new pair of denim jeans. He went into the change room to try on a pair of Levi's, which were way too tight for him. Somehow, carelessly, he pulled up the zipper really fast and caught the skin of his penis. After many attempts at unfastening it, plus a few concerned inquiries from the male shop assistant, he gave up. It was impossible to undo.

He put his jacket on, covering the offending part, and walked out of the dressing room, saying angrily, "I'll take them." The shop assistant apologized to Yellow Jacket, saying he would have to take them off just for a moment so that he could release the special little antitheft clip that sets off the door alarm. Furious but desperate, he pulled his friend aside and reluctantly told him what he'd done. His friend, apparently choking back laughter, made the assistant turn off the alarm so they could leave the shop.

Yellow Jacket refused to go to hospital, so he was driven straight home. After several more painful attempts to undo the zipper, he finally took a pair of scissors and cut the jeans completely away, leaving only the zipper attached to his penis.

This story cracked up the whole room, including Yellow Jacket. I was desperate to laugh but stifled it with a lump of sushi, coughing and spluttering as it went down. The boss went on to tell us that Yellow Jacket had at one point given up trying, pulled on a pair of pants, and gone out for a drink. He drank almost a full bottle of whisky, then went to his girlfriend and asked her to remove the zipper.

It was difficult for the boss to carry on because the laughter in the room was so loud. He finished the story by shouting, "And he still has the scar to prove it. Come on, Toshi, show us your war wound."

The people nearest him shoved and slapped him affectionately on the back, and he fondly pushed them away. More drinks were ordered and others tried, unsuccessfully, to match the boss's story.

Removing myself from the scene, I looked out of the window into the manicured garden that was blanketed by the sun's golden light. In the background I heard their crude laughter.

Looking back into the room, I studied Yellow Jacket. He was maybe thirty-five or forty and poorly educated. I guessed he was probably from a dysfunctional or broken home. Recruits are usually lured into the yakuza in their late teens or early twenties. It was easy to see why they joined. The yakuza is a kind of surrogate family and gives them meaning and a sense of belonging. In a society where the group is of paramount importance, there's little choice for these young men. The prerequisites for gang membership were loyalty, trustworthiness, and to be beyond question. It was the expected conduct of all Japanese groups, but for the yakuza it was a matter of life or death. The yakuza were the most insular of groups. Outsiders were considered suspect.

"Hey, Gaijin-san, play shakuhachi," I heard a voice say.

This is what the boss had bought me here for, to show off to his peers. I removed my flute from its bag and walked to the far side of the room. There would be no acoustics with all this tatami, I thought. After some childish cheering, the boss shouted, "Kojo no Tsuki." I knew the piece and went straight into it. The flute sounded lifeless, without any spirit. I was just following commands, after all.

I finished to tumultuous applause. The boss then asked if I could play a *min'yo,* or folk song. I nodded and started to play.

This they liked and started clapping along. The boss was smiling proudly. Once again his honor was intact. He hadn't made a mistake bringing me here. At the end of the song the boss said, *"Vely goodo,"* which brought another round of rapturous applause.

With the sideshow over, the gangsters all returned to their adolescent bantering. The boss led the way with a sexist joke, shouting at the waitress and pointing to his crotch, saying it was her turn to play the shakuhachi. This brought the house down. He was having a very triumphant day.

I went back to the table, pulled the cleaning rag through my flute, and put it away. Yellow Jacket stood up, said, "Finish," and caught my elbow, trying to hasten my departure.

They had finished with me. There were a few inebriated good-byes, but most of the men had become engrossed in their own conversations again. I said nothing.

I was taken to the parking lot by Yellow Jacket and offered the equivalent of two hundred dollars. I shook my head, but he insisted strongly. Then he handed me his name card and tried to explain, as best he could, that if I needed anything during my stay in Tokyo to simply call the number on the card. He asked the restaurant's receptionist to call a cab to take me to the station and handed her some money to pay the driver. With a slight bow, he thanked me, turned, and left.

Chapter Seventeen
Paying My Respects

It was the beginning of autumn, and the tail end of typhoon number thirteen was moving across the city heading north. The carriage was crowded and smelled musty. Condensation covered the windows on the inside, and rain splattered against them on the outside. The train traveled east towards Tokyo Station. From there I would catch a train to Shimoda, where five years earlier I'd visited the old komuso monk with Ozawa.

I stood in front of an attractive young woman who had been lucky enough to get a seat. She was fashionably dressed in the "career woman" look, right down to the little briefcase balanced on her lap. Long black hair, falling forward, screened her slightly from onlookers. Her lips were painted scarlet red, in sharp contrast to her chalk white face. To avoid wetting her clothes, she was daintily holding her designer umbrella with an outstretched arm. No part of the offending object touched her, and at her feet a pool of water steadily grew around its metal point. Her face and eyes were locked into an expressionless stare, a mask of blankness. Yet every time I looked away from her I could sense her staring at me. Each time I tried to catch her, she glanced away, and her expression reverted back to the porcelain mask.

Four stops from the terminus a foreigner got on, pushed his way through the crowd, and squeezed in next to me. Brushing water from his clothes and dripping on everyone, including the young woman, he said, "Hi, how're you doing?"

I knew immediately that he was from the States, for there is surely no other nationality as friendly to a stranger as an American in a foreign country.

"Fine, thanks. How about you?" I responded easily.

"Not so good," he said, waving his half-folded English newspaper, which was opened to the apartment section and had circles drawn all over it.

"I've been up and down this line looking for a place to live since early this morning. There's nuthin' out there, man. Well, nuthin' I can afford. The money they're asking for these rabbit hutches is ridiculous," he said dejectedly. "We've got closets bigger than them back home."

Sympathizing with his predicament, I listened as he went on to tell me how he'd been living in a noisy gaijin house for two months and was desperate to find a home of his own.

"I'll take anything at this point, man," he said.

The young woman, unable to resist, now sneaked glimpses at the two foreigners. She'd be much easier to catch now. *Got you!* I thought, as our eyes met. With no other option, she gave an angelic smile and slightly bowed her head in submission. She was probably wondering how it was possible for two strangers to make an acquaintance so quickly. Japanese didn't take the making of new friends lightly, as more acquaintances meant more obligations, more dinner dates, weddings, birthdays, funerals. Less space in their appointment book.

After establishing where I was from and, briefly, what I was doing in Japan, the American told me that he was from California. He had arrived in Tokyo during the sweltering month of August. Looking half-pleased and half-amused, he said he'd found himself a teaching job at a well-known language school in the city and, laughing, added sarcastically that the job was more like being an entertainer than a teacher. His plan was to stick it out for two years and make enough money to pay his way while he studied martial arts.

He was twenty-eight years old, handsome, well-mannered, and instantly likable.

Curious to know where I was off to, I told him I was going to Shimoda on the Izu Peninsula.

"So what's in Shimoda?" he asked

"I'm going to visit a temple," I said.

"That's a long way to go to see a temple. It must be special," he concluded.

"Yeah, it is," I said as we pulled into Tokyo Station.

The conductor announced that the train would be terminating and we would be exiting through the doors on the left side of the carriage. He listed off every line that was available from Tokyo Station, then reminded us that we shouldn't forget our belongings, giving a special mention for umbrellas. During the journey he'd also reminded us not to open the windows as this carriage was air-conditioned, and to hang on as we rounded a bend. At each station he had warned us of the potential dangers when disembarking the train. Japan Rail held our hands throughout the entire journey. There was no need to think. I remembered what the head monk had said several years ago at the Zen retreat: "Monk learn all rule. No need mind. Only eat, drink."

With the passengers now moving at a rushed pace, I quickly said good-bye to the American and wished him luck in his hunt for an apartment.

It had been two weeks since Ozawa called to tell me of the death of Ota Sensei, the old komuso monk. He had died suddenly, six weeks ago, while Ozawa was away on a business trip in New York.

Ozawa and I met for dinner to remember the monk and catch up on each other's lives.

"I missed a dear friend's funeral," said Ozawa, bitterly, "and I didn't see him before he died. The thought of it is too much to bear. He was one of the most important people in my life. In the last few months, I put this stupid job before our friendship."

"It couldn't be helped, Ozawa-san. You didn't know he was going to die," I said, trying to ease his pain.

"No. I have no excuse. I should have gone to see him before I left for the United States."

Ozawa seemed to be trying to drown his sorrows by consuming several drinks with dinner. Fortified by the alcohol, he began opening up, voicing his dissatisfaction with work and life in general.

"I've had enough of this way of life; I hate the bloody company," he said, becoming more morose as the evening progressed.

"Can't you ease up a bit at work? Then maybe you can see things more clearly," I suggested.

"I wish it was as simple as that," he said. "You know Japanese society well, Ray-san, but only from the outside. 'Easing up' is not a Japanese concept. We can't even ease up when we have a day off. You know that. I feel trapped. There's nothing I can do. This society is cruel, Ray-san."

"You really believe that there's nothing you can do?" I asked, somewhat harshly. "Look, Ozawa-san, we've known each other a long time now so I think I can . . ."

"And you still call me Ozawa-san," he interrupted, knowing that something serious was about to be said.

From the first day I'd met Ozawa at the Zen retreat, I had called him by his family name. It stuck, and I couldn't get used to using his given name.

"Look, *Norburo,*" I said. The very mention of his name made us both laugh, "Look, you can't go on blaming things outside of you. You're making yourself sick. Why don't you take a fresh look at what's going on here?"

"Yes, I know, I know. I need to make some changes in my life," he said.

"Be careful, Ozawa-san. People change 'things' all the time to escape from their unhappiness. They change their partners, their jobs, their homes, their cars; they even change their image. If we don't examine and understand the underlying cause of our unhappiness, then the changes we make will only be temporary, and we'll just keep moving from one escape into another, more appealing escape. The misery will still remain unexamined and unchanged."

"But you told me you changed the way you were living in London. You said you let go of a lot of the nonsense."

"Yes, that's true. But the lifestyle I let go of wasn't really the problem; it was just a distraction from the problem. The problem was, I had filled the emptiness with all kinds of nonsense as you say. I didn't know who the hell I was beneath the layers of bullshit. When I started getting glimpses of this sad and meaningless image I'd created, it was as if I was waking from a bad dream. It wasn't a question of moving from one thing to another, or a question of whether I should change. I could no longer hide from who I was. The negative had been exposed, so to speak. I could no longer carry on the way I was living. Change was choiceless."

"It's not as easy as that, Ray-san. Sometimes you have no choice but to carry on the way you're living."

"But have you looked to see if this is the case for you, Ozawa-san? Just take a look at what's really going on. Just take a look at what's behind all your misery. You won't find any answers outside of you."

"I wouldn't know where to start, Ray-san. There's so much for me to look at. Where to start looking is the problem."

"I started by looking at why I always blamed outside influences and the system for my unhappiness and troubles. I saw that by blaming something outwardly, I wouldn't have to face my fears and insecurities. I wouldn't have to look at the meaningless way I was living."

"We have to go about our business, Ray-san. We have to earn a living. I have no time to look into these things."

"Yes, you do. That's just another excuse that we use so we don't have to look at ourselves. Just take a look at what's really going on in your own life. See if you're getting some peculiar pleasure or some reward out of this destructive way you're living. If you are, you probably won't stop. You'll talk about change, make it into a hobby. You may even try to find someone to help you, but deep down you won't change if you're not really serious. Seriousness is its own change, Ozawa-san."

"What you're saying, Ray-san, reminds me of a Zen story. Perhaps you've heard it. It's about a monk who somehow, during the night, got lost in the monastery and fell out of a window. Fortunately, he was able to grab the sill and hang on for dear life. After a short while, the pain became unbearable, and there was no choice but to let go. He fell, only to find he'd been hanging merely three feet from the ground."

"Yes. It's a good story, Ozawa-san, and a good example. But he didn't really let go though, did he? He couldn't hang on any longer."

As we left the restaurant that evening, I told my friend I had decided to go to the old monk's temple in Shimoda after the long weekend.

"You're welcome to join me," I said optimistically.

Sadly, he declined, saying that he wanted to but would be out of town that week on business.

Standing in the middle of the station now, with my eyes busily searching the huge automated timetable for trains going to Shimoda, I heard the young American's voice call out to me.

"Hi, again! What time's your train out?" he asked.

"There's one every twenty minutes," I replied.

"Do you have time for a coffee before you go, then?"

"Yes, sure."

"By the way, my name's Perry."

"Ray."

Tokyo Station was teeming with people, and through the exit the city looked dismal. I looked out at the sheets of rain. Every second, colorful umbrellas burst open and floated towards a line of waiting taxis. The rain splattered on the hoods of the cars, making a terrific noise. Turn signals flashed vividly in the dimness of the day. Through the rain, I could see the neon sign of a café.

"Head for the pink sign," I called through the crowd to Perry. "I'll meet you there if we get separated." Pushing our umbrellas up, we started wading through the masses. The wind was blowing the rain in a sideways direction, making our umbrellas virtually useless. We arrived at the café with soaked shoes and trousers. At the entrance, we pushed our umbrellas into an already-bulging holder.

"We'll be lucky if we leave with the same ones," Perry said. It was true. Umbrellas seemed interchangeable in Tokyo.

We lined up for our coffee and then started looking around for a seat. The cashier said there were two more floors. I noticed a sign that said the third floor was a nonsmoking area. Nonsmoking areas were almost unheard of in Tokyo. We couldn't believe our luck.

"Nonsmoking! Great! It'll be empty," Perry said. "Have you ever seen people smoke as much as the Japanese do? Like cigarettes are essential, like food. The people don't seem to know about the health risks. Like they don't care if it shortens their lives. The cigarette companies must be making a killing here."

"Literally," I said, and we laughed at his choice of words.

"I guess health's not an issue here yet," he said.

"It didn't have to be before the American fast-food invasion," I commented wryly.

While we stood and waited for a table, I told him of the time I taught English to the president of Ajinamoto. This company produces, among other things, monosodium glutamate, MSG. In one of the lessons he tried to convince me that this product was not only tasty but really healthy as well. He said it was a vital part of the Japanese diet.

"No shit," said the American, laughing loudly.

We took sips from our Styrofoam cups and waited. A group of girls in navy blue uniforms stared at us, covered their mouths with their hands, and broke into a fit of giggles. Two of them got up from their table and joined their friends at another table. Again, this was performed to a chorus of giggles. Perry shook his head and looked skyward. We sat down, thanked the girls, and then tried to ignore them. One of them caught Perry's attention.

"Excuse me, your country please?" she squeaked.

"America," he said, then quickly, not allowing the conversation to continue, turned and spoke to me.

He made his living teaching young students, so he didn't feel like talking to them in his free time.

"If you could hold a gorilla down long enough," he said laughing, "and manage to get a shirt on its back and a tie around its neck, it could teach English here. I've met guys who boarded the plane to Japan as janitors and forty-eight hours later were 'Language Consultants' in downtown Tokyo. The language schools should advertise for performers, not teachers. That's what most of the students really want."

I laughed as he grumbled on. "You know, sometimes when you walk into a classroom and the girls all start collapsing about like idiots, as if you're some goddamn film star," he said. "God, it drives me crazy."

Grinning, I said, "Some people have miserable lives." This made us both laugh enough to draw the attention of the girls again.

Perry had first and foremost come to Japan to study Aikido with one of the great masters. He was taking a two-year course and upon completion would receive some sort of certification. This was not just any old Aikido but Ki Aikido, he said. This, he informed me, involved moving an opponent's ki energy to disable him. The image of Perry moving the intangible ki amused me, but to be fair, I think he meant working with an opponent's ki rather than physically moving it.

Four years earlier in Los Angeles, Perry had embraced the martial art of Aikido at one of the hard-core clubs in the city. The training was strict, traditional, and orderly, and the etiquette impeccable. Perry said he'd been attracted by the austere Japanese style of training and had become interested in the *bushido* code of conduct, as taught by the club.

Bushido was the ethical code of Japan's famed warrior class. The code combined physical, mental, and spiritual training to achieve the samurai's unbelievable level of mastery. The main principles of this code were benevolence, honor, wisdom, trustworthiness, and propriety. This was still the fundamental standard of conduct that ran through the seam of Japanese society.

Most non-Japanese get their first taste of these warrior virtues by watching some of the old samurai movies, the famous *chanbara*-style films featuring the exaggerated skills of the Shogunate swordsmen, as portrayed in Akira Kurosawa's *Seven Samurai, Rashomon,* and *Ran.*

After Perry earned his *shodan,* or first degree, in L.A., he read a book about Ki Aikido and immediately liked the idea of developing this mysterious untapped energy source called ki. The best teachers were in Japan, the book said. So without hesitation, Perry made arrangements to study with one of the great masters.

Two months later, he was sitting in a coffee shop telling me that his life didn't measure up to his image of studying in Japan. He wanted bushido discipline and the "Japanese way," but found only atrocious standards, a dismal atmosphere, and a lackadaisical way of training.

"There's about fifteen other foreigners at the *dojo,*" he said. "You can't believe the ego of some of them, man. They strut around like they're in some goddamn Kurosawa movie, with this 'don't fuck with me' attitude. You know the look, the really sour face and the walk like they've just shit themselves. It seems that the more skillful they get, the more egotistical they become."

I asked him why he stayed, and he said he was sure that the main teacher and a couple of the serious students had the "goods." Eventually, he hoped, they would pass on what they knew. He was determined to give it his best and stay the full two years.

Like so many people who had come to work and to study in Japan, Perry had arrived with an image that was entirely different from reality. I'd often meet foreigners on the train who came to Japan with a kind of coffee-table book vision of the country. The worst were the "adulators," who were excessively devoted and full of adoration of all things Japanese. They went on endlessly about how safe and clean it was in Japan, and how polite the Japanese people were, how "wonderful" everything was. At the other extreme, were the "detractors," who were only in Japan for the money. They mistrusted the Japanese, had no interest in the culture whatsoever, and saw insincerity in every Japanese smile.

Before Perry and I left the coffee shop, I told him there was an empty room in my building. It wasn't much, but it was cheap.

"I'll take it," he said with a laugh.

"Well, wait until you see it first." I said, handing him the address and the landlord's number. "Give the guy a call, and he'll show it to you."

We said our good-byes, and I headed back to the station.

Clutching a box of the most perfect purple grapes as a gift for the housekeeper, I approached the temple. A young man carrying freshly cut flowers from one building to the next caught sight of me and stopped.

"Good morning. May I walk around?" I asked.

"Yes, of course. Please do," he said.

I followed the narrow path that meandered through the garden, then walked back towards the temple and paused under the boughs of an almost bare tree. Only a few leaves clung to its branches.

I thought about Ota Sensei. I had met him only once, although I'd always sent my best wishes through Ozawa. A couple of times I had resisted the urge to come down and show him how well I was doing on the flute. He would have seen through that.

The advice the old monk had given me about the shakuhachi had always stayed with me. At first I hadn't been able to truly grasp the depth of his words—I was still trying to fathom the mystery of how to simply get a bloody note out of the thing. But as the years passed, and with each new breakthrough, I began to appreciate and understand what he had so passionately talked of that day.

He hadn't been wrong about the great discipline needed. I doubted whether one could be any kind of an artist without it. I was still learning about discipline, a discipline that isn't motivated by success or failure and where effort and hard work are their own reward and come naturally, without resistance.

Still, under the tree in the temple garden, I laughed as I remembered how amused the monk was when I told him that I'd only gone to the Zen retreat as a tourist.

The housekeeper I'd met so long ago appeared and caught me smiling at the memory of the monk. We greeted each other, and I apologized for not calling ahead. Then, not wanting her to feel pressured, I added that Ozawa had telephoned me and told me the sad news.

"He died peacefully in his sleep during the night," she said sadly. "He hadn't been ill at all. In fact, he seemed quite happy on the days before his death." She put on a brave face, but you could tell there was a void that only a short time ago had been filled by the monk.

Realizing I was still holding the grapes, I handed them to her. She thanked me and said she would make tea. She showed me into the same room where I had first met Ota Sensei. Removing my shoes and donning slippers, I entered through the sliding doors. There was a slight musty smell so the door was left open. Rays of sun streaked the room with yellow light. I sat in silence, enjoying the warmth of a sunbeam and picturing the monk sitting across from me scolding Ozawa, warning with a wave of his finger that he was wasting his life with all that business nonsense.

The young man I'd met earlier in the garden came in and apologized for disturbing me.

"Goto-san, the housekeeper, told me you visited here once before and were a shakuhachi player. Do you still play?" he asked.

"Yes, I do. Do you play?"

"Yes," he said, shyly.

"Were you a student of Ota Sensei?" I asked.

"Yes."

He told me that he had been a student of shakuhachi for five years and lived in Shimoda. In his spare time he helped take care of the temple grounds.

"Will you stay on at the temple?" I asked.

"I'm not sure what I'll do yet." He quickly changed the subject. "Did you bring your shakuhachi today?" he asked.

"Yes, I did. Actually I was hoping to play a piece today in memory of Ota Sensei," I explained.

"Perhaps you could play after you've had tea," he said.

"Yes, I'd like to. Thank you. By the way, my name's Ray."

"Honda. Pleased to meet you, Ray-san. Goto-san told me you're a good friend of Ozawa-san," he said.

"Yes, I am."

"Did you meet him through Sensei?" Honda asked.

"No. We met at a Zen retreat," I said.

"Oh really. Were you studying there?"

"No, not really," I said. "I was just there as a tourist."

Chapter Eighteen
Live at the Mokuba-tei

Awakened by what felt like a sizable earthquake, Dianne and I sat up, looked at each other, and uttered the word "Earthquake?" The old pre-war wooden apartment building had somehow, to this point, survived the ravages of time. It was flimsy and could easily have been torn down with bare hands. It wouldn't stand too many more tremors. On numerous seismic occasions Dianne and I had rushed for the street, certain we were experiencing the big one. But this time, nothing was going to bring us out into the freezing December weather.

While we worried about the building falling to pieces, the telephone started to ring.

"Get it, Ray. It'll be for you."

"No, it won't. It's never for me. You get it."

We pushed, coaxed, and sweet-talked each other into venturing from our cozy hibernation. The phone kept ringing. The room was so cold our breath hung in the air. Dianne finally succeeded in persuading me to crawl under the quilt to the bottom of the bed, where the phone was within reach.

"*Mushi mushi.* Hello," I said.

"Hi, this is Aki."

"Who?"

"Akikazu Nakamura."

"Oh! Hello, Sensei, I didn't recognize your voice." This was the first time he had ever telephoned me.

"Did you feel the earthquake?" he asked.

"Yes. It woke us up."

"Ray, I have a concert coming up in Tokyo on New Year's Eve. Are you free that night?"

"Yes, I'd love to come along," I said, thinking his invitation strange. Nakamura had never called about his concerts before. I always found out about them from Keino-san, his secretary.

"Good. I was afraid you would be busy that night. We will play 'Shika no Tone,' so please start practicing it before your next lesson. Oh, and by the way, it's an all-night concert, so there will be many other performers on the program."

Panic hit me. He wasn't asking me to come and listen. He was asking me to come and play alongside him. I could hardly believe it. New Year's Eve was just under a month away.

"Sensei, I'm not sure that I understand. You want me to play with you?" I asked in disbelief.

"Yes, of course!"

"But I don't think I'm ready, Sensei," I blurted out. Suddenly I felt the weight of duty on me.

"Don't worry," he said calmly. "You'll be fine. There's plenty of time to rehearse. We still have four weeks to go. I'll see you at our next lesson, Ray. Bye." He hung up.

I crawled back under the quilt and explained the missing parts of the conversation to Dianne.

"He's telling you something, Ray. He wouldn't ask you if he didn't think you were ready," she said encouragingly. "It's a fantastic opportunity. You'll be ichi-ban, Ray-san."

Four days after the call, I was on the train to Nakamura's studio, listening to "Shika no Tone" for the umpteenth time on my walkman. I knew the piece well but had never played it as a duet.

My fellow passengers were giving me sideways looks as I followed the Japanese music from the score on my lap. The music was written in two parts, one part for the stag and one part for the doe. Nakamura hadn't told me which part I would play yet, but I assumed the doe, so had highlighted that part with a yellow pen.

The first lesson was a confidence builder, with Nakamura assuring me that I was ready and that I could do it. Trying to allay my fears, he said he had learned and memorized pieces for concerts in twenty-four hours. The Japanese are masters at memorization, their whole education system largely depending on it.

We played it only once that day, and he said I should come three times a week until the night of the concert.

The rehearsals were quite different from my lessons because we had a deadline to meet. There was more nervous energy firing, with a real urgency on my part. Nakamura pushed me harder than usual and expected more of me. I loved it, and my learning curve took on new momentum.

The day before the New Year's Eve concert, we had one final rehearsal together. I played the piece right through without looking at the music. I was ready.

The concert was being held in Asakusa, one of the older, more traditional sections of Tokyo, close to the famous Asakusa Sensoji Temple. This part of the city had once been famous as a thriving "pleasure" and entertainment district and still retains the same energy and reputation to this day. Some of the most exclusive *geisha* houses still existed in the area, tucked away behind the facade of a wooden fence or a tiny tree-covered passageway.

The train to Asakusa was packed solid with people, many dressed in their New Year's finery. New Year's Eve is the one time of the year when the trains run all night in Japan. Arriving at Asakusa's subway station, I found that the area had been organized into roped-off passageways with white-gloved officials directing the thousands of temple goers with loudspeakers. I shuffled my way with the crowd, climbing the steep steps up from the underground.

Many Japanese choose to celebrate *Ganjitsu,* or New Year's, by visiting either their local temple or one of the larger, more famous temples in their city. They go to pray and make wishes for the coming year, and to give money in support of the temple. Naturally, the most auspicious time to be there is at midnight. The atmosphere at this time is one of camaraderie and fun. The temple grounds turn into a festive fairground with food and gift stalls set up. There are games for the children and hot sweet *amazaki,* which is thick rice sake, for the adults. Many of the ladies go to great lengths to dress up in their finest and most dazzling winter kimonos for the event.

In the big temples, thousands line up to ring the temple bell, pray for health and happiness, and throw money into the donation box. While there, it's customary to buy a variety of lucky charms from the temple stalls. These are kept for only one year, then returned to the temple at the next New Year's celebration. The amulets are then symbolically thrown onto a large bonfire in the temple grounds.

I once read somewhere that a staggering three million worshippers visit the popular Meiji shrine in Tokyo during each New Year's period. The donations and the sale of lucky charms must add up to an incredible amount of yen.

Surfacing from the station, I looked for Nakamura. The concert didn't start until 10:00 PM, so he had suggested we first meet for a bowl of *soba* noodles. We soon found each other and made our way to a tiny hole-in-the-wall restaurant. As etiquette demands, we noisily slurped our steaming bowl of hot noodles at high speed. No time for chat when you're eating noodles in Japan. After complimenting the "noodle master," we quickly vacated our seats, ready for the next person in line. Noodles are a traditional part of the New Year's Eve celebrations, and, at this time, the noodles are generally served uncut in very long lengths. The length symbolizes long life.

We walked for a few minutes through the crowds; then Nakamura pointed across the street to an old decorative building. He said it was the concert hall.

"It's one of the oldest music hall theaters left in Japan, Ray. It's called Mokuba-tei," he said.

The entrance had a tiny old-fashioned ticket booth at the side and was dimly lit by a couple of clear glass lamps. Above the entrance was a row of lanterns. As we made our way inside, I could smell the wonderful age of the building. The wood and polish mingled together, and as we entered the communal dressing room there was a pleasant smell of new tatami matting.

I was well aware that I was entering a world where few foreigners had set foot. I felt grateful that the shakuhachi had, once again, gained me access into an area of Japanese culture that I otherwise would not have seen.

Two female performers greeted us as we entered. One was kneeling on the ground looking into a long mirror. In front of her was a large makeup box filled with pots of colored creams and powders and brushes in every length. Her hair was flattened and netted in readiness for the huge black wig on the stand next to her. She was expertly painting tiny red lips onto her ghost-white face. A towel draped around her neck protected her clothes. The other woman was being helped into a gorgeous silk kimono that had cranes, rising suns, and the auspicious pine tree on it.

"*Ohayo gozaimasu,*" they greeted us in unison.

"Ohayo gozaimasu," we replied.

Nakamura explained that *ohayo gozaimasu,* normally a morning greeting, was used by theater performers as a greeting at anytime of the day.

On the low table in the middle of the room were a teapot, several cups, two large thermos jugs, and several boxes of tissues. In the far corner of the room were three older men, who, judging by the long cases lying on the floor beside them, played the shamisen. Each was helping the other put on his traditional formal costume.

Nakamura and I looked at the roster that was pinned to the notice board to make sure that our time slots hadn't been changed.

"1:30 AM. Good." Nakamura looked pleased. "You know that's the busiest time, Ray."

The entire concert was scheduled from 10:00 PM to 6:00 AM. The audience could buy tickets at any time between these hours and stay as long as they wanted if seats were available.

I sat on the dressing-room floor and made myself as comfortable as possible, a little daunted by the long night ahead.

As each performer arrived, there were enthusiastic shouts of "Ohayo gozaimasu." I got the impression that this must be a rule of theater—the louder and more irritating, the better. Perhaps to say it quietly would imply that you weren't fully involved.

As show time neared, the room filled up quickly, the "ohayo's" grating a bit by now. The shamisen players busily tuned their instruments, their twangs filling the room. Nakamura pointed to one of them and said that he was one of the best players in Japan and ranked number one in his particular style.

Two other shakuhachi players arrived and immediately took an interest in me. We introduced ourselves, and they handed me their name cards. Ranks needed to be established. These cards are an essential part of Japanese etiquette, as they immediately inform each party of the other's status. Without this information, the Japanese find themselves at a loss, not knowing who should defer to whom or what level of language to use. I had no name card to offer them, so they looked to Nakamura for a quick history.

One of them said he was looking forward to hearing me play. He was sure, he said, that I must be a great player to play alongside Nakamura Sensei.

"No, no, no. I'm just a student," I said, not meaning to sound Japanese but trying to defuse their expectations a little. It didn't work. They shrugged my protestations aside and insisted I must be great. Oh well. They would still say I was, even if I fluffed the performance.

The promoter arrived to more loud shouts of "Ohayo gozaimasu." He looked stressed and unhealthy and had dark circles under his eyes. His hair was dull, and he smelled heavily of cigarettes. I guessed he was a two-pack-a-day man. Bitterly, to anyone who was listening, he said someone had canceled at the last minute and he had been on the telephone for an hour looking for a replacement.

Nakamura greeted him and quickly introduced me. Seeing my foreign face seemed to give the promoter temporary relief from his problems. Smiling broadly, he grasped my hand firmly. "How do you do?" he said in a voice that seemed to come from the bowels of his body.

I returned his greeting in Japanese and said that he must be very busy tonight. He seemed to panic, perhaps thinking I would break into English at any second.

"English no, English no," he repeated, then began waving his hand under his nose to emphasize the no.

Looking back at Nakamura, he said he thought I was the first foreigner to have ever played in this theater. I smiled and thanked him for the opportunity.

Feeling a little better adjusted to my surroundings, I decided to wander around. The narrow corridor between the dressing room and stage was buzzing with activity. A couple of stagehands squeezed past me, carefully carrying a *koto,* which is a thirteen-stringed harp. A deliveryman wearing white hurried by, carrying four bowls of noodles on a tray. I walked onto the small stage and peered through the curtains. There was already a good crowd waiting noisily, some drinking sake and eating from disposable *bento* boxes.

At precisely 9:55 PM there was an accelerated series of clacks from the *hyoshigi,* two rectangular blocks of wood hit together to get people's attention. The show would soon begin. Dianne and I became familiar with the sound of the hyoshigi when we moved into our little Japanese room. In the wintertime we'd hear the sound through our window late at night. Going outside to find out what it was the first time we heard it, we were amused to see firefighters walking through the neighborhood. The clacking sound reminds people to turn off their gas stoves or anything else that might cause a fire in the event of an earthquake or otherwise.

With the sound of the hyoshigi, the promoter returned to the dressing room to offer a few words of praise and encouragement to all that were there. He said, "Gambatte," bowed, then went out onto the stage to give a very long introduction. Nakamura said we had lots of time, so he suggested we walk over to the Asakusa Sensoji Temple. We quietly left through a side exit.

Moving through the crowds, we passed the brightly lit food and gift stalls. The main avenue that led directly to the temple was lit by old-fashioned lanterns. After a few minutes of our shuffling along at a snail's pace, Nakamura pulled me from the dense mass and onto a tiny side street. We wound our way through several alleys and finally arrived at the temple.

Standing off to the side, we watched as hundreds of worshippers lined up to pray and make their New Year's wishes. People waited patiently, then, when it was their turn, they climbed the steps to the front of the temple to alert the gods by shaking a rope that was attached to a cluster of bells above.

When they had the attention of the gods, they tossed coins into a large wooden box, clapped their hands twice, and said a prayer. There were showers of coins aimed at the box coming from as deep as thirty feet back into the crowd. Huge sheets caught the coins that missed the box.

We walked over to a large bonfire and watched people throw their old charms into the flames.

The bushes and trees nearby were flowered with narrow strips of white paper tied to the branches. The strips are called *o-mikuji,* and contain a written fortune.

"If I buy one of these strips of paper, I can find out what my fortune holds for the coming year," Nakamura said. "If it gives me bad news, I can tie it to the branch of a tree to ensure that the bad fortune doesn't follow me home."

"That's very convenient," I said, laughing.

Because we didn't have to be back at the concert hall for at least an hour, we bought some hot drinks and found a place to sit away from the main festivities.

I had always enjoyed talking with Nakamura because he was so relaxed. Having lived and studied music in America for several years, he was accustomed to being around foreigners and found it easy to talk openly.

When we heard the first strike of the huge temple bell, we stopped talking. Its solemn deep, rich tone rang out along with every other temple bell in Japan. It was midnight, and this special bell would be struck one hundred and eight times by a giant, wooden log-shaped clapper. Under the guidance of a monk, the log, supported from the ceiling by thick ropes, would be swung by the temple visitors.

I had seen this ritual several times before, but had forgotten exactly what the one hundred and eight strikes symbolized, so I asked Nakamura to explain.

"We call this custom *joya-no-kane.* In Buddhist teachings, it's generally said that there are one hundred and eight worldly passions. So by striking the bell, we hope to dispel them all."

I told Nakamura that a Tibetan monk in India had given me a rosary strung with one hundred and eight beads. Each bead was carved into a skull. Later, I found out that this number represents the one hundred and eight desires and one hundred and eight illusions created by humans.

"Yes," he said. "It's the same. This custom must have come to Japan from India through China."

"Besides the rosary, another reminder I have of the old Tibetan monk is my shakuhachi bag," I said sentimentally. Nakamura looked puzzled. "In fact, the shakuhachi bag I gave you last year has the same Tibetan origins."

Nakamura, curious, asked me more.

I explained that, while in India, Dianne and I had become rather fond of an old hermit monk who had retreated into the mountains way above Dharamsala. We first met him by chance when we were hiking though the area. It suddenly started to hail massive stones that hurt when they hit, so we dashed for cover under a tree. An old monk clutching a basketful of pinecones saw us and yelled something over the noise of the storm. Beckoning us with his hand, he guided us along a narrow tree-covered trail. A scruffy white dog who'd been tagging along with us all morning followed close behind.

Within moments, we arrived at a small, mud-walled hut and were quickly ushered inside. Grateful to be out of the storm, we thanked him by placing our hands together as if in prayer. He smiled, said something in Tibetan, and quickly organized us onto two small wooden stools. He then began filling the pressure cooker with water. Pumping the stove several times, he lit the flame and set the pot to boil. He was making us Tibetan butter tea.

As our eyes adjusted to the darkness, we could see that the tiny cell-like room was simply furnished. He had a narrow bed, a small wooden table, a large metal storage box, a primus stove, some blackened pots, and a few dishes. Near his bed was a small colorfully decorated Buddhist altar. Pinned around it were several faded postcard pictures of the present Dalai Lama and a photograph of the monk standing next to him.

While waiting for the water to boil, he came and sat on his bed opposite us. He looked about sixty years old, but it was hard to tell. His robe was completely threadbare and had several hand-sewn patches across the knee area and hem. Feeling around the bed, he picked up a rather thick-lensed pair of the popular Dalai Lama look-a-like glasses and placed them on the end of his nose. Dianne, circling her face and pointing at him, said he looked like the Dalai Lama. This made him beam, and although he was missing many teeth, his smile lit up the dingy room.

The pressure cooker started hissing steam. He removed his treasured glasses, got up, mixed the ingredients for the salty butter tea, and allowed the brew to bubble for a while. Dianne and I had been forced to drink this type of tea while on a trekking trip in the Himalayan region of Ladakh in northern India. It was pretty bad to our taste and actually made us gag on contact, but here it was impossible to refuse; the frugal monk had used his precious supplies to make us the most buttery rich tea possible.

Carefully, the monk wiped out three tea bowls with a section of his dirty, tattered robe. Then he strained the tea, transferred it into a large Chinese thermos jug, and served us each a bowl full.

Dianne, thinking she was clever, allowed the tea to cool so she could gulp it down in one go. Our friend generously refilled her cup immediately! Smiling, I slowly sipped on. Remembering that we had some cookies and fruit in our daypack, I quickly fished them out and offered them to the monk.

Now that we were all comfortable, the monk brought out his beloved photographs to share with us. Before opening the old album, though, he ceremoniously pulled on a very old, moth-eaten saffron cape. Slipping his glasses back on, he was ready to enter his old world. There was an old picture of the famous Potala Palace in Lhasa, Tibet, and another of a young monk standing outside a monastery. Pointing to the monk in the picture, he said it was he.

There were also several photos of a very young Dalai Lama and some more recent ones of him standing, sitting, and walking. With each picture, the monk placed his hands together reverently. Noticing that my cup was almost empty, he quickly topped it up. As he leaned forward to pour, I noticed deep red scars on each of his wrists.

I pointed to his wrists and mimed someone in handcuffs. He nodded his head and began telling us about his imprisonment and escape from Tibet. Along with his Tibetan words, he mimed the events. His arms moved as if he was running and looking over his shoulder. Then he mimed a person with a stern looking face pointing a rifle at him. He mimed being hit in the mouth, and he showed us his broken teeth. With an expression of sadness, he threw his arms up in the air. They had caught him.

He lifted his arms in front of him, grasping two imaginary prison bars. He looked sad behind the bars. Pulling his robe off his shoulder, he showed us more terrible scars on his back. He spoke the word *Nepal* and pointed to his callused feet, indicating that he had walked from Tibet. Then he raised his arms into the air in triumph. For some reason I raised mine too. We toasted this tragic hero and downed our butter tea.

After this meeting, whenever we hiked up into this area, Dianne and I always took him some supplies—usually some rice and sugar or a bag of tea and some clarified butter. Dianne always made sure he got some fresh fruit and vegetables as well as candles and sometimes kerosene. On one of our visits he presented us with his one hundred and eight bead rosary. We tried desperately to refuse it, but he insisted, leaning forward and pulling our three heads together affectionately.

Two weeks before we were due to leave Dharamsala, Dianne came up with the brilliant idea of having a new robe made up for our friend. He desperately needed one. Not wanting to offend or break any rules, Dianne asked our old friend Tenzing for advice. He said he was sure it would be most appreciated and told Dianne which tailor to go to in the town.

With the approximate measurements in hand, Dianne purchased burgundy and saffron material from the fabric shop. She delivered it to the tailor with instructions to make two undershirts and one robe. Four days later, we picked up the finished garments. With the burgundy and saffron remnants that were left, Dianne instructed the tailor to make up three long shakuhachi bags.

Hiking up to the monk's hut for the last time on our trip, we felt excited and also a little nervous about giving him the gift. We worried that it might embarrass him and make him feel indebted to us in some way. But he was delighted and accepted the gift with an open and uncomplicated heart. The monk made us feel so happy we wanted to cry. Through mimed actions, we told him we were soon leaving India.

He made us tea, and we shared our last bowl together. As we said good-bye, he held our hands together in a pile and brought them to his forehead. We, in turn, did the same, taking this humble man's rough and damaged hands into our own.

I told Nakamura that of the three shakuhachi bags, I kept one, gave one to Yokoyama, and had one for him. He thanked me again for his Tibetan shakuhachi bag and signaled that it was time for us to head back to the concert hall. Instead of going straight to the dressing room to change, we entered the theater's auditorium. Standing silently at the back, we watched as an exquisitely dressed woman glided across the stage to the twang of the "number one" ranked shamisen player. She danced and dueled in time to a storm of dissonant notes, occasionally pausing to listen and look, her eyes peering over the upper half of her fan. Each time she stopped her knees bent, pulling the material of her kimono taut, creating a sensuous curve under her buttocks. Then, with her feet never leaving the ground, she would retreat across the stage again. The plucking of the shamisen became more aggressive, the dancer more threatened. She looked in distress. A jarring last note shuddered into silence, finishing the piece. The dancer obediently came to a halt, bringing the audience to their feet.

There were only a few vacant seats in the theater. My stomach tightened for just the briefest moment when I saw Dianne and two of her friends among the crowd. I'd played in front of thousands of people during my time busking, but I'd never "officially" played in front people of I knew.

"Ray, let's go and change," said Nakamura. "We are on in twenty minutes."

Back in the busy dressing room, invisible screens automatically went up around us as we changed, Nakamura into a formal kimono top and skirtlike, wide-legged *hakaman* pants and I into a freshly laundered white shirt and dress pants. Unwrapping my flute, I placed the two parts together, carefully lining up the holes, then blew a series of warmup notes that clashed horribly with the tuning up of a *biwa,* which is an Eastern lute, on the other side of the room. Nakamura gave me the nod to go. I hastily pulled my cleaning rag through the barrel of the flute, feeling more like I was loading a musket than preparing for a concert.

Standing in the wing, I listened as the Master of Ceremonies announced our names and told the audience that we would play "Shika no Tone" on shakuhachi. The applause began.

"Please," Nakamura said as he pointed the way on stage. Taking a deep breath, I walked out, and, without looking at the audience, found my place. With the sight of me, the applause became supportively louder for a moment. I smiled. Nakamura soon came on stage and positioned himself about ten feet away from me.

The clapping ceased, and on Nakamura's cue we both bowed. He then stepped forward and explained that I was a student of shakuhachi. He repeated my name and said I was from England. After this he announced the piece, then, like a restrained performer in a classical Japanese *Noh* drama, he gracefully glided back into position. We both bowed again, and the audience resumed its applause.

Nakamura raised his flute ceremonially into position. Then, with a pause that seemed to last forever, silence filled the auditorium. As Nakamura blew the first mournful sound of a lonesome deer crying desperately for its mate, I felt the same adrenaline rush as when I'd first watched him perform this piece.

I listened and waited. Then, raising my flute in the same ceremonial way, I readied myself. For the briefest moment, my mind went tormentingly blank. Then somehow, hearing my cue, I returned the lonesome deer's call. The exchanges came and went perfectly. The last month's hard work was truly coming together. I was playing well and felt good. Nakamura's powerful cry was calling out to me once again when, without warning, a man in the front row leapt from his seat and started yelling excitedly and pointing in my direction.

Oh god! I thought. Distractedly, I watched him while waiting for my next cue. He was definitely drunk, and I could only guess that he'd slept through the introduction, and, when he awoke, his disbelieving, bleary eyes focused in on me. Overcome with the shock of seeing a gaijin playing shakuhachi, he came to stand right below me, pointing and clapping.

My cue, my cue. As if in slow motion, Nakamura's head turned slightly towards me. *I was in. No harm done.* As I played on, I was able to watch the drunk quite calmly. Flopping forward onto the chest-high stage, he good-naturedly showed me his upturned thumb, wiggling it in several directions. He then reached into his pocket and pulled out his wallet. Spilling the contents onto the stage, he picked out a thousand yen and threw it towards me, blowing the note to help it on its way.

Turning to the audience, he raised his clapping hands, trying to encourage everybody to join in. Thankfully, two men caught hold of his arms and ushered him back to his seat. I somehow completed that section of the duet and passed it back to Nakamura.

We moved through the final difficult sections, Nakamura definitely sounding like the more powerful buck and me the weaker doe. Our separate melodies progressively overlapped, eventually becoming more alike until we were finally united in perfect harmony. Following the ending of the last note, we held the silent flutes to our mouths for a moment longer, then removed them and bowed.

Again the drunk in the front row leapt from his seat, turned to the audience, and, like a conductor, started wildly applauding. The crowd joined in this time, and soon the drunk had the audience members out of their seats, giving us a standing ovation.

Back in the dressing room, Nakamura warmly congratulated me on my playing. He then commented on the drunk and said that I had shown remarkable calm during the interruption.

Finally able to laugh about it, we had fun doing a play-by-play of my admirer's performance.

I saw Dianne standing with her friends in the foyer. I stood and watched her for a while. She had the same vivaciousness that I'd seen on our first meeting at the art gallery in London. I walked over, and she greeted me as warmly as a newlywed, wished me a happy new year, and then told me how thrilled she was by my playing. We all laughed about the drunk, and her friends said they felt terrible for me up there. They sympathized that I had to stay until the end, then said they were all off to watch the festivities at Sensoji Temple.

By 5:00 AM the acts were still going on with the same fervor, even though there were only about twenty or thirty people left sitting in the audience. Those in the audience who weren't sleeping or dozing were most likely supportive family members and friends of the final performers.

Obliged by custom to stay until the end, I watched right up until the last act and then headed to the dressing room. The artists who had other musical commitments that night had already left, but the rest of us sat quietly on the floor with our backs against the wall.

The promoter came in to say the concert was over. He gave a speech and thanked us all. Then he asked us to join him in a rousing synchronized clapping routine, where everyone in the room joined in and clapped out a well-known rhythm. Then we bowed to each other and said our good-byes.

Feeling tired but exhilarated, I gathered my belongings and walked out into the bright morning sun of a new year.

Epilogue

In April 1995, on a cool, sunlit morning, I boarded the Express train at Narita Airport and disembarked, an hour and a half later, at Shinjuku Station in downtown Tokyo. I was alone. Dianne was in Victoria, British Columbia, Canada, our new home. We had emigrated there soon after we left Japan. I would be in Tokyo for three weeks this visit. Dianne, who, on previous trips usually joined me, couldn't make it this time, due to commitments and studies. Among other things, she has plunged herself into an extremely demanding style of yoga called Ashtanga and is practicing daily. We keep our winters free of engagements so that we can disappear into the foothills of the Himalayas for four or five months each year.

Thanks to the many contacts I've made while living overseas, I have built up a small concert circuit in Japan, which affords me three or four visits annually. This particular visit was special. I had recorded my first compact disc and was excited to give copies to each of my teachers and friends. And I was heading south after Tokyo to stay with Ozawa-san. I hadn't seen him for two years, although we had talked on the telephone. Ozawa's life had, happily, changed for the better, though, sadly, it had not been of his own doing. He hadn't run away and joined a monastery, as he had once half-jokingly wished, but ironically, had been made redundant when the company he worked for was dissolved after being caught in one of the many corruption scandals in Japan. He was now running his aging uncle's tourist inn in Kyoto and had never been happier.

My first performance was arranged for the following day with Akikazu Nakamura. Nakamura was there to greet me when I arrived at the concert hall. We would support Ms. You Izumo, one of Japan's great traditional dancers. The piece she would dance was called "Toki." The *Toki,* otherwise known as the crested Ibis, was considered one of the most revered birds in Japan, but due to hunters, these magnificent creatures were gradually disappearing. Izumo-san told me that there were only two old Ibises remaining in Niigata prefecture.

Izumo-san would dance a requiem to a dying Ibis shot by a hunter. The piece, she said, depicted the happiness of the female bird as she flies across the countryside with her mate and then the sorrow after he is shot. The female, grieving the loss, kills herself by thrusting her bill deeply into her own chest. Throughout the performance, the flutes would improvise and add another dimension to the emotionally charged atmosphere.

Just before the concert began I handed Nakamura my CD. I hadn't told him I had recorded it, as I wanted him to be surprised. He looked at the disc, went quiet, thanked me, and then carried on with his business of directing stagehands and making sound checks. His cool reaction gave me the impression that he was a little upset with me, perhaps for not consulting with him first. Maybe he thought it pretentious. He said no more about the CD that day.

Three days later, I was booked with Nakamura again, this time at his shakuhachi school's recital near Roka Koen in the western suburbs of Tokyo. Each student would play a folk, jazz, or honkyoku piece in front of a packed house full of friends, relatives, and paying guests.

Nakamura announced one student after another, then went and sat in the front row to listen. When it came to my turn, I walked on stage and Nakamura followed. He announced my name to the audience and told them that I had emigrated from England and was now living in Canada. Then he said that three days ago I presented him with a gift that had left him speechless. He had left it until this moment to express his gratitude. He instructed one of his students, who was sitting in the front row, to hand him my CD. I stood beside him, feeling a little uncomfortable and embarrassed as he explained about my former life in London, about my serendipitous meeting in the grounds of a temple with his teacher Katsuya Yokoyama, and about how I had busked to pay my way while studying in Japan. He went on to tell them how I made my living now through teaching shakuhachi and giving seminars and performances in Canada, the United States, and Europe. He held out the CD.

"This is the result of Ray-san's diligent efforts," he said.

The next day I didn't have any engagements, so I did what I loved best on my visits to Japan. I caught the train to Takeo-san, hiked up the mountain to my cedar tree, and played shakuhachi.

Glossary

All Japanese words that appear in *Blowing Zen* are translated when first introduced. After that, if the word is repeated, the reader may consult this glossary.

Amazaki	Thick rice sake
Ban-cha	Rough grade of Japanese tea with less caffeine
Bento	Food box/container
Biwa	Eastern style lute
Bushido	The code of the warrior
Chanbara	Samurai-style movies
Daijobu	It's okay
Dam-e	Not good/Do not do it
Dojo	Practice/training hall
Domo arigato gozaimasu	Thank you very much
Dozo	Please
En	Inevitable connection or fate
Fuke	Zen Buddhist sect associated with Komuso
Furukusai	Stinking of old
Futon	Thin sleeping mattress
Gaijin	Outsider/foreigner
Gambatte	Persevere/Never give up/Study hard/ Go for it/Make a strong effort/ Do your best

Epilogue

Ganjitsu	New Year's
Gomen kudasai	I'm sorry to bother you/May we come in, please?
Hai	Yes
Hajime mashite	How do you do?
Hakaman	Name of wide legged-pants
Hanami	Cherry blossom viewing
Hara	Vital energy center of the body
Honkyoku	Original pieces
Honto	Really, is it true?
Hyoshigi	Two rectangular blocks of wood, which when hit together make a clacking sound
Ichi-ban	Number one
Ichi on jobutsu	Enlightenment in one sound
Irasshaimase	Welcome
Jinkoh	Type of aromatic wood
Jo stick	Long hardwood pole
Jouzu desu ne	Very proficient
Joya-no-kane	Buddhist custom: Striking of temple bell to symbolically relieve world of the hundred and eight worldly passions/desires
Kaihogyo	One hundred–day marathon
Kampai	Used when drinking: Cheers
Kanji	Japanese written characters
Katakana	Japanese writing system
Kawai so	Poor thing
Ki	Energy or spiritual strength
Kinhin	Walking meditation
Koan	Paradoxical dialogue

Koban	Small local police station
Koboku	Aromatic wood
Kohdo	Appreciation of incense
Komibuki	Musical breathing technique: pumping the diaphragm to create an unrefined vibrato effect on flute
Komuso	Monks of nothingness and emptiness
Konichiwa	Greetings/Good day/Hello
Koto	Thirteen-stringed harp
Kudasai	Used for polite requests
Kumiko	Incense game where one identifies different types of incense
Ma	Meaningful silence between sounds
Madake	Type of bamboo: Phyllostachys bambusoides
Min'yo	Folk songs
Miso	Fermented soybean paste
Mushi Mushi	Hello
Muzukashi	Very difficult
Nakodo	Matchmaker
Noh	Classical Japanese dance-drama where masks are worn
Nori	Light seaweed
Ohayo gozaimasu	Morning greeting
Ohisashiburi desu ne	Long time no see
Oishi	Delicious
Omanek domo arigato	Thank you for inviting me
O'miai	Arranged marriage
O-mikuji	A written fortune sold at temples
Pachinko	Game similar to pinball
Ro	Musical note

Glossary

Ronin	Masterless samurai
Roshi	Enlightened Zen Master/Head abbot
Sake	Rice wine
Sakura	Cherry blossom
Salariman/men	Office worker(s)
Samue	Traditional Japanese work clothes, consisting of baggy pants and short kimono-style jacket
Samurai	Member of warrior class
San	Added to end of name out of respect
Satori	State of higher consciousness
Sayohnara	Good-bye
Seiza	Seated position with legs folded under you
Sembei	Rice crackers
Sensei	Title of respect/Used for professionals
Sento	Japanese public bath-house
Shakuhachi	Japanese bamboo flute
Shamisen	Three-stringed Japanese lute
Shodan	First degree
Shodo	Calligraphy
Shoganai	Nothing can be done/What's done is done
Shojin-ryori	Zen temple food
Shugendo	Ascetic path to realization
Shugyo	Spiritual exercise
Soba	Noodles
So desu ne	I see
Sugoi	Wonderful/Amazing/Very good
Suizen	Blowing Zen/breath control
Sumi-e	Traditional black ink painting

Sumi-masen	Excuse me
Taki-shugyo	Waterfall training
Tatami	Thick woven reed matting
Tengai	Beehive-shaped woven reed hat that covers whole head and rests on shoulders
Tofu	Soybean curd
Toki	Crested Ibis
Torii	Traditional gateway to temple or shrine
Wakarimasen	I don't understand
Yakuza	Japanese mafia
Yama-bushi	Ascetic mountain dwellers
Yoroshiku onegaishimasu	Pleased to meet you (polite form)
Yubitsume	Ritualized removal of tip of little finger as a punishment
Yukata	Cotton kimono
Zazen	Formal sitting meditation in cross-legged position
Zendo	Zen meditation room or hall

List of Musical Pieces

"Ajikan"	"All Is emptiness/Emptiness Is Form"
"Amazing Grace"	(No translation needed)
"Haru no Umi"	"Spring Sea." Famous composition by Michio Miyagi.
"Honshirabe"	"Original Piece." Often played as a prelude to a larger piece.
"Kimigayo"	Japanese National Anthem
"Kojo no Tsuki"	"Moon Over the Castle"
"Koku"	"Empty Sky." Considered one of the most ancient and important pieces in the shakuhachi repertoire. Played by the komuso with the aim of attaining the ultimate state of enlightenment.
"Rokudan"	Traditional piece in six parts.
"Sagariha"	"Falling Leaves." Depicts the wind blowing through a bamboo grove.
"San-an"	A prayer for the easy delivery of babies.
"Sanya"	"Three Valleys." The three high points in the piece suggest the struggle towards enlightenment.
"Shika no Tone"	"Distant Cry of the Deer"
"Tamuke"	"Offering." Commemorative piece for the dead.
"Tsuro no Sugomori"	"Tenderness of the Cranes"

List of Recurring Characters

For concerts, talks, or seminars, contact:
www.raybrooks.com

The CD of the music mentioned
in this book is available from:
www.newalbion.com

or

New Albion Records, Inc.
PMB525
584 Castro St.
San Francisco, CA 94114

🌹 ALSO FROM H J KRAMER

Way of the Peaceful Warrior
A Book That Changes Lives
by Dan Millman
A spiritual classic! The international best-seller that speaks directly to the universal quest for happiness.

Beyond Fear
Twelve Spiritual Keys to Racial Healing
by Aeeshah Ababio-Clottey and Kokomon Clottey
Teaching that racial healing comes about through personal transformation, *Beyond Fear* offers readers twelve spiritual keys with which to explore their beliefs and feelings about racism.

The Life You Were Born to Live
A Guide to Finding Your Life Purpose
by Dan Millman
Dan Millman's popular Life-Purpose System features key spiritual laws to help understand your past, clarify your present, and change your future.

Diet for a New America
How Your Food Choices Affect Your Health, Happiness, and the Future of Life on Earth
by John Robbins
In this new edition of the classic that awakened the conscience of a nation, John Robbins brilliantly documents that our food choices can provide us with ways to enjoy life to the fullest, while making it possible that life itself might continue.

All titles are available at your local bookstore, or by calling (800) 999-7909. For a free book catalog, please send your name and address to: H J Kramer, P.O. Box 1082, Tiburon, CA 94920.

✴ Children's Books From
H J Kramer / Starseed Press

Available Spring 2000
My Spiritual Alphabet Book
by Holly Bea, Author of *Where Does God Live?*
illustrated by Kim Howard
This lively book teaches self-esteem and joy while educating young
children on the basics of the alphabet.

Secret of the Peaceful Warrior
by Dan Millman
illustrated by T. Taylor Bruce
The heartwarming tale of one boy's journey to courage and
friendship. Recipient of the Benjamin Franklin Award.

Where Does God Live?
by Holly Bea
illustrated by Kim Howard
Beautifully illustrated by best-selling artist Kim Howard,
Where Does God Live? is a fun way to introduce children to
the concept of a loving deity.

The Lovables in the Kingdom of Self-Esteem
by Diane Loomans
illustrated by Kim Howard
A delightful frolic through the animal kingdom that introduces
children to the qualities of a positive self-image. Also available in
easy-to-read board book format for younger readers.

All titles are available at your local bookstore, or by calling
(800) 999-7909. For a free book catalog, please send your name
and address to: H J Kramer, P.O. Box 1082, Tiburon, CA 94920.